Triathlete's Edge

Triathlete's Edge

Marc Evans

Human Kinetics

Library of Congress Cataloging-in-Publication Data

Evans, Marc, 1953-
   Triathlete's edge / Marc Evans.-- Rev. and updated ed.
     p. cm.
Rev. ed. of: Endurance athlete's edge. c1997.
Includes bibliographical references (p.) and index.
   ISBN 0-7360-4653-4 (pbk.)
   1. Triathlon--Training. 2. Endurance sports--Training. I. Evans,
Marc, 1953- Endurance athlete's edge. II. Title.
   GV1060.73.E93 2003
   796.42'57--dc21

2003000189

ISBN: 0-7360-4653-4

Copyright © 2003 by Marc Evans

Triathlete's Edge is a revised and updated edition of *Endurance Athlete's Edge,* originally published in 1997 by Human Kinetics Publishers, Inc.

The Web addresses cited in this text were current as of 2/24/03, unless otherwise noted.

Acquisitions Editor: Martin Barnard; **Developmental Editor:** Julie Rhoda; **Assistant Editors:** Carla Zych and Alisha Jeddeloh; **Copyeditor:** NOVA Graphic Services; **Proofreader:** Kathy Bennett; **Indexer:** Nan N. Badgett; **Permission Manager:** Toni Harte; **Graphic Designer:** Fred Starbird; **Graphic Artist:** Francine Hamerski; **Art and Photo Manager:** Dan Wendt; **Cover Designer:** Keith Blomberg; **Photographer (cover):** © Getty Images/Phil Cole; **Photographer (interior):** © Jeffrey Dow unless otherwise noted; **Illustrator:** Roberto Sabas unless otherwise noted; **Printer:** United Graphics

Human Kinetics books are available at special discounts for bulk purchase. Special editions or book excerpts can also be created to specification. For details, contact the Special Sales Manager at Human Kinetics.

Printed in the United States of America 10 9 8 7 6 5 4 3 2 1

Human Kinetics
Web site: www.HumanKinetics.com

United States: Human Kinetics
P.O. Box 5076
Champaign, IL 61825-5076
800-747-4457
e-mail: humank@hkusa.com

Canada: Human Kinetics
475 Devonshire Road Unit 100
Windsor, ON N8Y 2L5
800-465-7301 (in Canada only)
e-mail: orders@hkcanada.com

Europe: Human Kinetics
107 Bradford Road
Stanningley
Leeds LS28 6AT, United Kingdom
+44 (0) 113 255 5665
e-mail: hk@hkeurope.com

Australia: Human Kinetics
57A Price Avenue
Lower Mitcham, South Australia 5062
08 8277 1555
e-mail: liahka@senet.com.au

New Zealand: Human Kinetics
P.O. Box 105-231, Auckland
Central
09-523-3462
e-mail: hkp@ihug.co.nz

Contents

Preface

Triathlon made a dynamic impression with its debut at the 2000 Olympic Games in Sydney, Australia. The sport and I have come a long way since 1981, the year I began coaching world-class and amateur triathletes professionally. Now triathlon is recognized the world over.

Triathlete's Edge provides cutting-edge training drills and programs for the triathletes and triathlon coaches who are enthusiastic about the sport. In more than 20 years of coaching I have learned many lessons and have worked to become an expert in each discipline of the sport—the techniques and nuances of swimming, cycling, and running. This experience provides the background for the coaching techniques, drills for each discipline, and supplemental training that I recommend in part I. My years of working with many athletes also have fine-tuned the way I use periodization models, which are discussed in part II of the book. Periodization describes the general phases of training from base preparation right up to the competition, as well as the particular number of workouts for each sport each week, targets of these workouts, tests, specific intensities, training volumes, transition workouts, upper and lower body dryland training, stretching, and the specific types of intervals for each.

The book offers my most up-to-date triathlon training and coaching curriculum. You will find methods for physical self-assessment of muscle length (so important to achieving optimum ranges of motion and maintaining posture) and cutting-edge drills, techniques, and exercises for improving swimming, cycling, and running performance. Chapter 5, "Functional Strength and Triathlon Performance," contains exceptional information on core strength and stability and exercises developed specifically for triathletes. Novices to elite-level performers have become better triathletes by learning how to initiate movements with well-developed core muscles.

I have developed *Triathlete's Edge* over many years of coaching endurance athletes individually. One-on-one coaching has distinct advantages over coaching a group. With an individual, a coach can concentrate on the distinct training needs and biomechanical idiosyncrasies of that particular athlete. He can dedicate his time to fine-tuning the technique of one athlete instead of the general conditioning of several differently skilled athletes.

Triathletes will become better athletes by combining the study of the technique of each sport with coaching. The information presented in this book will help athletes educate themselves better about the sport; as well,

I recommend that athletes seek out competent and experienced coaches to enjoy improved triathlon performances. A book or on-line training program by itself won't hurt, but adding independent coaching on a regular or occasional basis is by far the best approach for the beginner to the elite triathlete.

I am grateful to triathlon for providing me a vehicle through which to express my love of coaching. From the 1980s to early 1990s I worked with some of the best athletes in triathlon, well before I had fully perfected my coaching style. Nowadays I work primarily with age-group triathletes with a broad spectrum of skill levels. And it is this work that is most satisfying and these athletes to whom I owe a great deal for allowing me to test my theories. I hope that, after reading and studying *Triathlete's Edge* and applying the fundamentals of the program, you enjoy the developments in your athleticism and achieve the success you seek.

Marc Evans
www.evanscoaching.com

Acknowledgments

In every respect, the Riekes Center for Human Enhancement in Menlo Park, California is devoted to providing an environment where individual interests and goals are unvaryingly important. The athletic facilities—including a swimming flume, track and running analysis treadmills, cycling assessment room, Olympic platform, and core and stabilization areas, along with physical therapy resources—are a coach's dream playpen. Because of the philosophy of the center and the people who work there, I have been able to develop my independent work in a most inspirational setting.

Over my 20 years coaching athletes, a few people have been of particular importance to me as friends, mentors, clients and colleagues: John and Carolyn Aver, Dirk Bartels, Ralph Black, Jeff Bortniker, Ken Burns, Frank and Julie Cadjew, Peter Cazalet, Guy Courtney, Dean Harper, Gina Kehr, Juliann Klein, Ferdy Massimino, Julie Rhoda, Gary Riekes, Greg Skidmore, Ned Spieker, Scott Tinley, Kathy Torgersen and, of course, Mom.

PART I

TECHNIQUE AND SKILL TRAINING

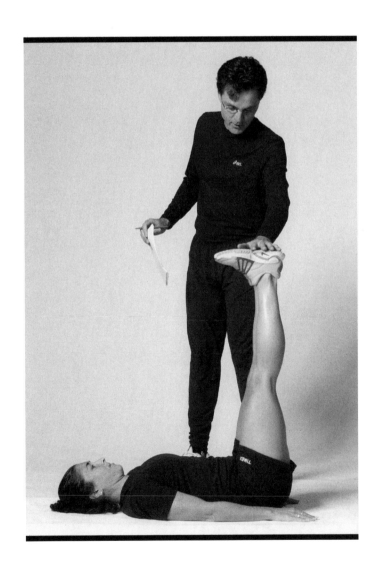

CHAPTER 1

Assessing Your Triathlete Physique

Every human being begins at birth a lifelong progression of biomechanical learning. An infant's motor skills are undeveloped, making the most mundane physical task for an adult a riddle for the child. There is magnificence to a toddler's unconditioned and often delicate endeavor to control movement, but learning its biomechanics takes time, growth, and neuromuscular development.

As children grow, they become more skilled at coordinating and stabilizing various complex movements. This neurological growth of motor control is important for the ongoing development of the coordination and efficiency of movement. Not surprisingly, what we become skilled at springs from our environment—what we're exposed to. From an early age we learn by ourselves and teach ourselves movement skills that contribute significantly to our athletic capacity as adults. As a coach, my aim is to teach adults how to improve movements in ways many have not experienced before.

Most triathletes work very hard and put in long hours of swimming, cycling, and running to improve their performance at their complex event, and many age-group athletes work just as hard and put in as many hours as the elite triathletes. So what makes the differences in performance so significant? There is a host of reasons—physiological, psychological, and experiential—that allows some athletes to be faster and stronger than others. While some of the psychological and experience-based gaps among athletes can be bridged by training and racing, there are limits to how much athletes can change the physiological differences among themselves.

One of the limits in physiological training is how much athletes can improve their maximal oxygen capacity—the maximal amount of oxygen the body can take up and provide to the muscles during exercise. After several years of consistent training, when an athlete's cardiovascular system is in shape, it is difficult if not impossible to further increase the maximal oxygen capacity. However, training *can* continue to change and improve an athlete's economy of movement—how economically her body uses oxygen, processes energy, and conserves movement. It is for this reason that so much of my work in coaching triathletes focuses on improving technique and economy of movement by increasing functional strength and flexibility. These three aspects of physical effort—technique, economy of movement, and functional strength and flexibility—are central to the program and training principles of this book.

Chapters 2, 3, and 4 address the first two aspects by providing concepts and drills that are useful for improving technique in swimming, cycling, and running, respectively. Improving technique makes movements more economical—less energy is used to go faster and for longer. Poor technique applied in any of the triathlon events undoubtedly increases oxygen costs and energy usage.

In this chapter, we focus on the foundational assessment and training for increasing functional capacity in strength and flexibility. Constructing a training program on a stable basis of physical support is essential for the triathlete. There is little doubt that supplemental, or what I call "dryland" training (what an athlete does to improve overall strength and flexibility), can make a recreational athlete better and a great athlete even greater. Triathletes perform supplemental dryland training to enhance performance, avoid and rehabilitate injuries, and maintain and develop strength (to counteract endurance training's reduction of muscular strength), power, muscular endurance, and flexibility.

The principal purpose of supplemental dryland training is to strengthen the supporting skeletal and postural muscles used in all three sports, lessening the chance of injury from overuse and improving the muscles' ability to stabilize movement. Running most notably requires a stabilized muscular system to propel the athlete forward, with each foot strike causing a considerable impact force to the foot that results in a muscular and skeletal chain reaction. Gait, foot mechanics, stride length and rate, and center of mass all play important roles in stabilization, but it is nonetheless essential that proprioception (movement sensory perception) and strength be tested to their limits. In *Better Training for Distance Runners* (Human Kinetics 1997, 281), David E. Martin and Peter M. Coe stress the importance to endurance athletes of supplemental exercise: "Such training can contribute to making the difference between winning and simply performing well, and between being injury-prone and injury-resistant."

A triathlete, of course, is not a runner, but a hybrid athlete—an endurance swimmer, cyclist, and runner combined. The endurance component inherent in triathlon training and competition and the unique blend of swimming, cycling, and running into one sport make the triathlete's physique unique. The long-limbed, barrel–chested, and narrow-hipped swimmer gradually becomes leaner with triathlon training. Skinny-armed cyclists training for triathlons build chest, back, and arm muscles; and sleek runners evolve into

© Martina Sandkuhler/Jump

In addition to sport-specific endurance training, a key to bettering your triathlon performance is to strengthen your core muscles.

proportioned physiques as they develop proficiency in the other two sports. Sooner or later, the characteristic figure of the triathlete appears as the muscular endurance and leanness develop. I have seen this happen before my eyes again and again as the triathlon training begins to take hold.

For ectomorphs, this transformation occurs rapidly, because their body type is suited for the "tri-ectomorphic" physique. These lean, sinewy athletes have the physical characteristics of the "well built." They are not too thin, overly muscled, or soft or round. For others, specifically those with mesomorphic (muscular) or endomorphic (rounded) body types, achievement of the triathlete's form is limited by genetics; but considerable improvement in physique and endurance can be made with the right training.

Body Posture: Perfecting the Body's Performance Position

Perfecting body posture is a fundamental, and perhaps even the single most important, part of becoming an efficient triathlete. Sagging, rounded shoulders and a hanging head restrict rhythm and balance and increase the oxygen debt during movement, whether it is swimming, cycling, or running. The musculoskeletal system is designed to maintain posture—the foundation of movement—and support body weight during movement. Therefore, posture and stabilization exercises for the muscular support systems are central to educating the athlete about body awareness.

Because every athlete is different, a "blanket" postural or musculoskeletal assessment cannot be made. Later in this chapter, we review parts of the musculoskeletal assessment process as performed in a physical therapist's evaluation. A few postural positions are essential for triathletes to be aware of as they train for competition. These essential positions are not to be used only when working out; they are even more beneficial if they become habitual in everyday activities, as well—from working at your workstation, driving, standing, rising from a bed or chair, bending over, and so on.

Remember these key postural points:

- Always hold up your chin (about three inches above your collarbone) while swimming, biking, and running. Try running or biking up a hill with your chin tucked in toward your chest and you'll see how much more difficult the effort becomes.

- Keep your back straight and your chest high (the high chin will help you with this). Running uphill is much more strenuous if you lean forward.

- Position your earlobes directly over your shoulders at all times while swimming, cycling, and running.

Adhering to these three key postural points during your daily training (and other activities) will help you maintain the musculoskeletal and anatomical functional positions that will improve your technique and elevate your performance (figure 1.1).

Once you have evaluated and are working to improve your postural position when training, it's time to work on the limitations of functional muscular strength and muscle length (flexibility) that may be holding back your performance. Functional strength permits the most effective and efficient performance of swimming, cycling, running, flexibility exercises, and dryland training.

Figure 1.1   Maintaining an athletic posture while training and competing—back straight, chest forward, and chin up—produces better biomechanics.

Assessing Functional Strength

A musculoskeletal assessment is a tool for determining the functional strength and flexibility a triathlete uses when swimming, cycling, or running. Its fundamental purpose is to ascertain how the athlete's posture, gait, mobility, muscle length (flexibility), muscle strength, and foot mechanics affect the performance. These assessment findings are then used to develop an individualized training plan.

Ken Burns, director of physical therapy at the Riekes Center for Human Enhancement in Menlo Park, California, treats most of my athlete-clients. After working closely with Ken (our offices are next door to each other), I discovered that for many of my athletes, undergoing a comprehensive evaluation of their musculoskeletal strengths and weaknesses (including flexibility) has a decided impact on their success.

A musculoskeletal assessment involves manual muscle testing that reveals flexibility, strength, and biomechanic patterns in the pelvic region, core, and lower and upper extremity musculature. The results point out muscle strengths and weaknesses, helping a triathlete identify the areas that need strengthening and learn how these muscles tie in with swimming, cycling, and running performance.

Muscle Imbalance and Athletic Performance

Ken Burns, PT, Director of Physical Therapy, Riekes Center for Human Enhancement

Muscle strength and its assessment are influenced by anatomical, physiological, biomechanical, and methodological considerations. Athletes and coaches often don't pay sufficient attention to factors that influence voluntary muscle contraction, such as the number of muscle fibers activated and the frequency and pattern of their firing. It is well known that the quality of muscular contraction, together with the sequencing of the activation of individual muscles during a particular movement, has a considerable influence on final muscular strength. However, many coaches and athletes presume that increasing muscle strength depends almost entirely on the quality and quantity of strength training. The truth is, there are many factors that can prevent muscles from being strengthened to the desired degree.

"Muscle imbalance" can be described as an altered relationship between muscles that are prone to tightness and muscles that are prone to weakness. This imbalance can develop to such an extent that it may become the primary limiting factor in athletic performance. Muscle tightness can develop without any structural problem or injury and can sometimes be associated with the overuse of the particular muscle or group of muscles. It creates a condition in which the muscle is shorter than its normal resting length.

Muscle tightness influences motor behavior in many ways. The most important are the following:

- Inhibition of the tight muscle's physiological antagonist—the muscle that opposes its movement. For example, tightness frequently occurs in the back extensors and hamstrings, preventing athletes with such tightness from achieving optimal strength in their abdominals and quadriceps until the length of the shortened muscles becomes normal.

- Muscle imbalances lead to an increased risk of injury and developing joint dysfunction over time. This is sometimes due to the overuse of muscles, tendons, and ligaments.

- Muscle imbalance leads to the development of abnormal or inefficient biomechanics for swimming, cycling, and running. It is often difficult to determine whether the muscle imbalance is the primary problem and the inefficient movement pattern secondary or vice versa.

Muscles that tend to develop tightness include the back extensors, hamstrings, hip adductors, gastrocnemius-soleus, hip flexors (iliopsoas, rectus femoris, and tensor fasciae latae), piriformis, quadratus lumborum, pectoralis major and minor, upper trapezius, levator scapula, and neck extensors.

More common weak muscles include the vastus medialis, abdominals, scapular stabilizers (serratus anterior, rhomboids, middle and lower trapezius), deep neck flexors, and ankle dorsiflexor (anterior tibialis).

Musculoskeletal assessment of an athlete can help the athlete and coach address existing muscle imbalances as well as prevent such imbalances from developing.

Flexibility and Endurance Performance

Flexibility is one of the most important (and most overlooked, misunderstood, and neglected) aspects of successful triathlon training and performance. Although absolute normal ranges of flexibility do not exist, the optimal completion of some athletic movements requires a specific range of flexibility. Using these ranges, a therapist can evaluate the limitations that exist and the improvements that can be made in the functional flexibility of the athlete.

There are many divergent biomechanical, physiological, and musculoskeletal variables that come into play in flexibility. As we've seen, in a musculoskeletal assessment the physical therapist evaluates and helps to guide the triathlete to achieving optimal flexibility, strength, and performance. All three of these elements, particularly the muscles' lengthening capacity, must be assessed at the joints pertinent to the movements of swimming, cycling, and running.

Ideally, I recommend that my athletes have a qualified orthopedic physical therapist conduct an evaluation of muscle length, because she will provide the most objective numbers. A 90-minute assessment costs around $210. The following paragraphs, however, review some self-testing procedures and specific stretches you can do to improve flexibility in various muscle groups. I also note how restriction within a particular muscle group may affect performance.

Hamstrings

The hamstring group includes three muscles located on the back of the thigh (biceps femoris, semitendinosus, semimembranosus). The hamstrings, the primary knee flexors, help to manage forward and backward movement. The semimembranosus and semitendinosus both originate on the ischial tuberosity and insert on the medial tibia. The biceps femoris has two heads. The long head originates on the ischial tuberosity and the short head on the femur. They both insert on the head of the fibula via a common tendon.

If the hamstrings' movement is restricted or tight, the triathlete compromises his ability to bend forward on the bike's aero bars and shortens his optimal running stride length. Obviously, both issues affect the economy of these movements and the overall performance. More important, this restriction of movement may also lead to injury due to the other muscles—the primary movers and supporting muscle groups—being overused to compensate for the shortened hamstrings.

Note that bending forward and touching the toes is not necessarily a good indicator of adequate muscle length in the hamstrings due to disproportionate leg (sometimes due to hamstring restriction), arm, and trunk lengths. A method for the general self-assessment of hamstring muscle length is shown in figure 1.2a. Unrestricted hamstring muscles will allow the athlete to achieve a 90-degree position (legs to floor) when the knee is straight. The self-assessment is a good place to begin, but I strongly recommend that a physical therapist conduct the evaluation. Figure 1.2b shows an effective stretch to increase mobility in this muscle group.

a

b

Figure 1.2 Hamstring assessment (*a*) and stretch (*b*).

Quadriceps

The quadriceps group includes four muscles in the front upper leg: the vastus lateralis, vastus medialis, vastus intermedius, and the rectus femoris. The quadriceps muscles pull on the femur to control the amount of flexion and extension at the knee.

When the quadriceps lack flexibility, they restrict anterior rotation of the leg (at foot strike, the quadriceps function eccentrically to decelerate the forces of impact), leading to patellar tendonitis in affected cyclists and overuse injuries and muscular imbalances in runners. Tight quadriceps muscles reduce stride length by lessening hip extension following push off, slowing the triathlete.

A self-assessment method for determining the quadriceps' functional range of motion is performed by sitting on a table with both legs hanging off the edge. Extend the right leg (figure 1.3a). Full extension indicates that the leg is normal.

Figure 1.3b illustrates a particularly effective method for self-stretching all four muscles of the full quadriceps group. Due to the nature of their sport, triathletes are predisposed to developing hamstring and quadriceps tightness, overdevelopment (leading to muscular imbalances), and reduced hip and knee ranges of motion. Stretching the full quadriceps muscles as shown improves on more commonly used stretches by elongating each quadriceps muscle during one stretch. The four muscles making up the quadriceps are powerful extensors for the knees.

a   b

Figure 1.3   Quadriceps assessment (*a*) and stretch (*b*).

Hip Flexors

The hip flexor muscles (iliacus and psoas major and minor) control hip extension while running. Poor flexibility in these muscles prevents full extension, shortening the stride length, which, along with stride rate, determines how fast one can run.

Poor hip flexor flexibility also restricts the gluteals (the powerful buttocks muscles especially helpful in cycling), reducing their contraction capacity. Swimming, cycling, and running mechanics and efficiency are impacted by restricted gluteals. In swimming, the kick requires hip extension to facilitate stabilization of the trunk. A limited range of motion likely reduces the ability to rotate around the axis, which means the triathlete will swim with "flatter" hips, thereby increasing his surface area and drag.

A tight hip flexor group (flexion and extension) can lead to low-back pain as well as increasing the lumbar curve—and that definitely isn't the functional athletic posture you're looking for. To self-assess hip flexor mobility for flexion, lie supine (on your back) and bring your right knee toward your chest; a normal range is about 120 degrees (figure 1.4a). For extension, lie prone (on your belly) and lift your right leg; a normal range of extension for this movement is about 30 degrees (figure 1.4b). Figure 1.4c shows an excellent stretch for the hip flexors.

a

b

c

Figure 1.4 Hip flexor assessment [(*a*) flexion, (*b*) extension] and stretch (*c*).

Piriformis

Anatomically, the piriformis muscle lies deep inside the gluteal (buttock) muscles; the sciatic nerve passes either beneath or through the piriformis. Injury to the hamstrings often causes sciatic irritation, which results in burning pain in the buttock, down the back of the thigh, and sometimes into the lateral calf and foot. If the latter locations are affected, however, there may be another reason for the pain, and undergoing a qualified medical evaluation is recommended.

In general, the piriformis is a lateral rotator of the hip joint, which also helps to abduct the hip if it is flexed. The function of the piriformis changes with the flexion of the hip, as in biking and running, and it is important to the stabilization of the hip and posture. Evaluation of tightness in the piriformis requires a therapist's evaluation of the lower back, hip, and thigh. Figure 1.5 shows a good stretch for the piriformis.

Figure 1.5 Piriformis stretch.

Groin-Hip Adductors

The adductors assist in stabilization, flexion, and lateral rotation of the hip, and flexion and medial rotation of the knee. They are the muscles in the upper thighs that pull the legs together when contracted. Although a triathlete is less likely than a hockey, basketball, or baseball player to sustain injury to the groin, it is nonetheless important to maintain the proper range of motion in this muscle group, which helps to stabilize the legs while running. To assess your own functional range of motion for hip adduction, lie supine and gently spread your legs (figure 1.6a). A 50-degree arc from the centerline should be possible with both legs. To stretch (figure 1.6b), lie supine and cross the right leg over the left, then pull the left leg outward against the right foot.

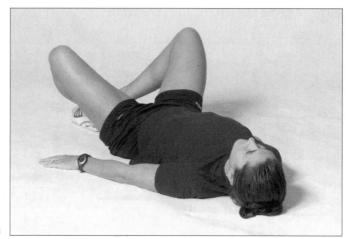

a

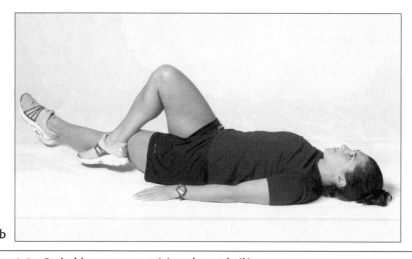

b

Figure 1.6   Groin-hip assessment (*a*) and stretch (*b*).

Gastrocnemius-Soleus

The gastrocnemius-soleus is gener-ally referred to as the calf muscle group, and it is located on the posterior side of the lower leg. Flexion of the knee and foot are among the key roles this muscle group plays. Restrictions in flex-ibility, and specifically of the muscle's ability to lengthen, will limit the pushing-off phase of running and "ankling" dur-ing the pedal stroke in cycling. Other muscles (called syner-gists) that support these muscles sometimes take over and cause early fatigue. An athlete with tight gastrocnemius-soleus muscles has a reduced range of ankle dorsi-flexion (flexion of the ankle so that the top of the foot moves toward the body) and increased pronation, leading to shin pain, plantar fasciitis (a painful inflam-mation of the fascia along the bottom of the foot), and other compensatory complications.

Self-assessment of gastrocne-mius-soleus flexibility is made by checking the plantar flexion (fig-ure 1.7a) and dorsiflexion (figure 1.7b) of each ankle. Plantar flex-ion is the pointing of the toes, and achieving about 50 degrees of arc is normal. Dorsiflexion of the ankle is performed by pulling the toes toward the shin; 20 degrees is within the normal range. Figure 1.7c shows an excellent stretch using a towel for resistance.

a

b

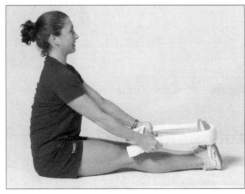

c

Figure 1.7 Gastrocnemius-soleus assess-ment (*a* and *b*) and stretch (*c*).

Shoulder Complex

The shoulders are stressed repeatedly in swimming. The thumb-to-spine assessment illustrated in figure 1.8 tests the adduction and internal-rotation range of motion of the shoulder complex. Place first your right hand behind your lower back and slowly move your thumb up your spine. Note the height achieved. Repeat with the thumb of the left hand. The goal is to achieve an equal range of adduction on both sides. Stop when you cannot go any farther up the spine or you experience any pain. Excessive restriction in the shoulder indicates posterior capsule tightness, which may cause shoulder tendonitis. Increasing the range of motion to a normal value may require manual stretching by a physical therapist, but the shoulder stretches described in chapter 2 may also help.

Figure 1.8   Thumb to spine assessment.

Latissimus Dorsi

The latissimus dorsi muscle extends, adducts, and medially rotates the arm and assists in shoulder flexion (drawing the shoulder forward and downward), internal rotation, and spinal flexion. Perhaps most important for swimming, this muscle extends, adducts, and medially rotates the humerus at the shoulder. The thoracic and lumbar muscle groups support the spine, but restricted or weak "lats" affect performance by limiting the range of motion and even causing back pain.

During swimming, the hands enter the water and the wrists flex downward and outward. At this time in the movement, the hand is positioned to "hold" the water in what has for many years been referred to as the catch position. It is here where the lats really come into play by helping to raise the body over the fixed hand.

In swimming, running, and cycling, the latissimus dorsi also aid postural stabilization. Inflexibility and muscular weakness in this area can lead to overuse compensatory injuries such as low-back pain. In addition, muscular weakness diminishes performance potential, so it is clear that this muscle, the span of which is the widest in the body, needs attention.

Muscle length in the latissimus dorsi is best evaluated by a physical therapist, who can objectively evaluate flexion, extension, and lateral rotation. However, if you cannot achieve 90 degrees of flexion (touching the toes with the knees straight), there's a good chance the latissimus dorsi and other thoracic and lumbar muscles are restricted or weak.

You will find some excellent flexibility exercises and drills for both the latissimus dorsi area and the shoulder complex in the following chapter, "Athletic Swimming."

CHAPTER 2

Athletic Swimming

The Achilles heel of many triathletes is swimming. In 20 years of coaching triathletes, I've given thousands of swimming lessons. Year after year, in lesson after lesson I have taught good swimmers to become better and poor swimmers to swim correctly. The core muscle group—including the abdominals, latissimus dorsi, gluteals, chest, and hips—plays a huge role in swimming. Combining stroke drills with proper biomechanical understanding and applications will help make every stroke smooth and streamlined. Finally, as discussed in chapter 1, improved muscle length and flexibility will also greatly assist in the execution of proper swimming mechanics. But perhaps what most enhances triathletes' efforts to swim better is using a swimming flume with instant video playback.

My ability as a coach to start and stop the flume at a moment's notice to give instruction and play back video of swimmers in the water (or underwater when the facility has the capacity; see figure 2.1) gives me an edge over coaches who must work in a pool. Although I use both flume and pool for evaluation, there is a decided advantage to using the flume early on. The coach and swimmer can review a flume tape several times in just a few minutes, so each coaching session includes dozens of replays and corrections to the swimmer's technique. Initially, I noticed that I was able to coach swimmers on a greater number of technical points of their stroke simply because I didn't have to wait 30 to 60 seconds while they swam an entire lap to discuss technique. Feedback and stroke correction are more immediate with a swimming flume, and having video playback allows a swimmer to view his or her technique and better understand how to correct it. The underwater views are of particular value in teaching swimming because the coach and swimmer can see the timing of the underwater stroke, hand pitch angles, body roll, and kick dynamics. You don't have to have a flume to improve technique, but if one is available, it will reduce the coaching and communication time and increase the speed with which swimmers can make significant improvements to their underwater stroke.

© Ken Redmond Photography

Figure 2.1   Swimming flume underwater photos can help you evaluate and correct your technique.

Coaching swimming technique is about teaching the athlete how to make the right movements to improve the efficiency of the stroke—that is, to get more distance from every stroke while using energy efficiently. To that end, each swimmer comprehends or feels her stroke differently. This makes teaching correct technique more difficult than simply following a checklist. First, I videotape a swimmer (preferably in the flume) from below and above the water, review the tape with the swimmer, and discuss with him the global aspects of his stroke. For example, a high percentage of triathlete swimmers have a tendency to initiate the underwater stroke too soon after entry, and many also have a low body position in the water due to inefficient stroke and kick mechanics. Taking the time with swimmers to describe the concepts behind these global faults is an important first step, and from there the process becomes very individualized as we work toward improving each mechanical flaw. Interestingly, a lot of swimmers who come in asking to work on their kick mechanics are surprised when we spend the whole session working on elbow position and hand pitch to improve their kick. The kick (I teach a six-beat kick, discussed later), which stabilizes the body in the water, functions better when arm, chest, and hand motions are enhanced.

What follow are the concepts of good stroke mechanics I've developed over several hundred swimming flume coaching sessions and over 20 years of coaching triathletes. For the most part, better swimming is achieved by training an athlete to perform to the best of her ability a continuum of skills (often by also working on other things, such as flexibility, muscle strength, and the ability of the muscles to take instruction from the brain). Fundamentally, I teach each swimmer to perform in the manner most suitable for them the above-water mechanics of the release, recovery, and entry as well as the underwater mechanics of the arms, chest-to-hip region, and feet.

Before we get into specific stroke mechanics, however, let us discuss a fundamental element of swimming that recently has become popular, although knowledgeable coaches have long known it to be of particular importance in successful swimming—use of the core muscles.

Core Strength and the Athletic Posture

You have the choice to swim more quickly and efficiently by using long swimming strokes and a larger mass of the body's musculature—the back, abdomen, chest, hips, and thighs, which collectively contribute more propulsion potential than, for example, swimming with the muscles of the arms alone. Using only small muscles when swimming produces ineffective, short, choppy, fast strokes and an inefficient, hasty kick.

Therefore, effective propulsion is produced by positioning the hands in the most "lift generating" position in the water while contracting the muscles of the body's core in a dynamic (concentrated) way. The speed of swimming improves quite a bit when a swimmer engages the core muscles and minimizes his dependence on the pulling action of the arm and hand through the water. The term "pull" in swimming misleads many swimmers into believing that they are to pull their hands through the water. Instead, the most effective hand motions are crosswise to the direction in which you are moving through the water. The hand anchors itself by sculling crosswise and the body then moves over the hand.

Doing this correctly calls for a strong core musculature in which the abdominal, back, and gluteal muscles assist body rotation to produce a longer, more propulsive stroke. Chapter 5 describes in detail how the triathlete can improve the functional strength of the core. Using the core muscles during swimming also enables an athlete to maintain an athletic posture throughout the stroke, which steadfastly supports athletic movement. Given that injuries occur more frequently in the presence of fatigue, it is critical for the stabilizing musculature of the athlete to be in top form. With improved endurance in the muscles that stabilize and maintain postural control, an athlete will tire less quickly and experience fewer injuries.

In simple terms, I tell my athletes to maintain a "core, trunk, and stabilized" position in every movement and sport. This is characterized by the athletic position (figure 2.2), in which the posture of the athlete is most stable. When swimming, this position sets up an effective propulsive phase that then is accomplished by strong contraction of the core muscles. Timing is also enhanced because a balanced core contributes to the efficacy of stroking, rotation along the axis of the body, and kick stabilization.

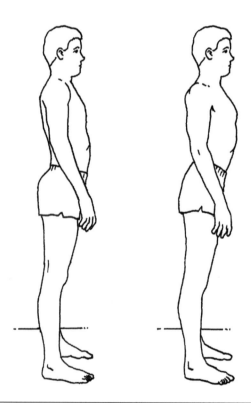

Figure 2.2 Untrained (left) versus athletic (right) posture.

Better Freestyle Mechanics

Learning better swimming mechanics starts by breaking the freestyle stroke into its specific stroke phases: release and recovery of the hand and arm from the water, entry and extension of the hand and arm into the water, and the underwater stroke—the catch and upsweep. In this section, a series of drawings depict each of these phases (see figure 2.3) and, along with the text that accompanies them, helps to establish clear objectives for performing better strokes for more efficient swimming.

Release and Recovery

The release and recovery phases of freestyle swimming span the part of the stroke in which the hand exits the water at the thigh (release) and then reenters the water in front of the shoulder. When exiting the water, the little finger comes out first. The arm is straight initially, ensuring a full extension to the thigh, and then the elbow slowly lifts while the forearm and hand hang loosely down. I coach almost all of my athletes to learn this type of release and recovery. (Only if the swimmer has a limitation in shoulder or back muscle flexibility do I teach a straight-arm recovery.) It's also important that the timing of the strokes on both sides be similar to balance the mechanics of the stroke.

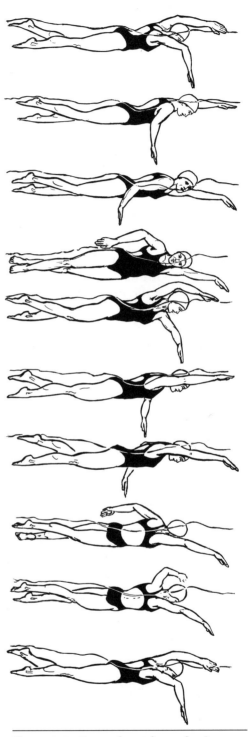

Figure 2.3 Proper freestyle mechanics.

Reprinted, by permission, from Cecil M. Colwin, 2002, *Breakthrough swimming* (Champaign, IL: Human Kinetics), 51.

These two methods of executing an out-of-water arm recovery can be used without affecting the triathlete's swimming speed or efficiency. The traditional recovery, commonly called a "low hand, high elbow" recovery, is performed by carrying the hand low alongside the body with the elbow high (figure 2.4). The second method, reserved for less-flexible swimmers who cannot perform the technique as just described, is the "high hand, low elbow" recovery, in which the arm exits the water straight until the hand comes near the head. The forearm and hand then relax and fall toward the shoulder prior to the entry (figure 2.5). If the sides of the stroke are unbalanced, the swimmer may need to engage in facilitated stretching with the help of a physical therapist or trainer to improve the range of motion.

Swimming in open water during a triathlon is altogether different from swimming in a pool. The wave action, narrowed swimming space, and fatigue that can accompany open-water swimming are good reasons for a triathlete to learn both recovery methods. The low hand, high elbow recovery is good for smooth water conditions; in very choppy conditions, the swimmer should present the most streamlined body position possible, and the high hand, low elbow recovery minimizes the frontal surface area for the waves to impede by reducing the wideness of the shoulders.

A fine way to learn the low hand, high elbow recovery is to drag the fingertips across the top of the water when swimming freestyle.

© Empics

Figure 2.4 High elbow, low hand recovery.

Figure 2.5   High hand, low elbow recovery

Entry and Extension

At about one-half of an arm's length beyond the shoulder, the hand, with the thumb leading, enters the water at a 30- to 45-degree angle just inside the shoulder. The wrist, elbow, and then shoulder pass through an imaginary hole made by the index finger and thumb as the hand enters the water. Extend the arm, but continue to keep the elbow slightly flexed (not hyperextended). It is very important that you be able to see the tip of your elbow at full extension. This keeps your head forward and streamlined in the most functional position and lengthens the stroking arm and body roll along its axis.

Underwater Stroke

One of the more difficult parts of the freestyle stroke to learn is the part that occurs under the water, particularly the catch phase in which the hand and forearm anchor into water that is not moving in a backward direction. When the hand moves diagonally across the body, it is this still water that anchors the hand. As you know from doing a chin-up, pulling your chin to bar height isn't easy because your body weight dangles below that level. Imagine the swimming stroke as a similar movement, except that each arm works independently, anchoring into the stationary water under the body (an imaginary bar) and pulling as the body moves over this stationary bar. That's what really happens when you're swimming more quickly and efficiently.

Water moves backward as a result of a movement of the hand against the water, and swimmers should steer clear of this backward-moving water. Put simply, a swimmer should feel water pressure on the hand at all times during the stroke. This requires the hand to frequently change its angle of attack. A good rule is to point the fingertips downward for much of the underwater stroke. This helps maintain the water pressure on the hand and increases propulsion and forward momentum. Swimmers often place too much emphasis on pulling or pressing down and backward with the hand during this catch phase. In other words, they focus on pulling rather than on finding the optimal hand, forearm, and elbow positions in the water.

World-record swimmers exhibit an efficient catch in the water by keeping the elbow and upper arm high—just under the surface of the water—during the entry. The catch is executed by internal rotation of the upper arm (rotating the biceps inward) while the elbow flexes to about 90 degrees and the armpit is open. To learn how to do this on dry land, stand facing a wall with your arms raised overhead, wrists flexed, and fingertips touching the wall surface. Now, slowly slide your fingertips down the wall toward your thighs. Your elbow will remain high, flexed, and easily positioned at 90 degrees. This high elbow position places the hand in the water in the optimal position, engages larger muscles, and achieves a remarkably strong and athletic core position during the middle and late stages of the stroke.

Once the hand and forearm are back in the water, positioning them for the most efficient entry and catch can be accomplished by following these steps.

1. After the hand and forearm enter and are just under the water's surface, extend them until you can see the tip of the elbow. To do this, gently rotate the hand, forearm, bicep, and shoulder inward. (While this happens, your other hand is entering the exit or "release" phase from the water into the recovery phase.)

2. The hand and forearm in the extension phase then should fall downward and slightly outward, with the thumb's leading edge beginning and directing the movement. At this time, there should be little, if any, downward movement from the elbow to the upper arm. This important movement positions the hand in still (nonmoving) water. Let the hand and forearm fall while keeping the upper arm and elbow at the surface until the hand is almost directly under the elbow. Perhaps the best visualization is to picture keeping your armpit open by pointing your elbow upward to lift your arm.

3. In this leveraged position, the hand is anchored in still water and the body is in an anatomical position advantageous for using the larger core and trunk muscles for propulsion, reducing stress on the shoulders and smaller muscle groups.

Triathletes should try to achieve this hand position during the catch phase, which I believe to be the most important part of the stroke. It is there that balance, propulsion, and momentum interconnect and set up the rest of the stroke. You do not need to press or pull aggressively with the arms. Instead, the technique described allows the hips to rise and the kick to become more fluid, which increase the distance realized per stroke.

Many triathletes are surprised to learn that during the underwater stroke after the catch phase, the hand moves diagonally across the body with subtle changes being made to its pitch and angle of attack. This crosswise hand movement begins with the catch. A skilled swimmer does not pull her hand backward at this point in the stroke, but rather uses diagonal sweeps to enable the hand to anchor in nonmoving water. This anchoring of the hand produces a propulsive force and considerably improves lift, efficiency, and swimming velocity.

The thumb side of the hand predominately leads the direction, angle, and speed of movement during the stroke. Thinking of the thumb side as the leading edge of a wing may help you visualize why leading with the thumb is important. When a wing is propelled through the air, there is an upward force on the wing due to air passing more quickly over the top of the wing than beneath it. The pressure this produces on the upper surface (the top of the wing) provides the lift. Air deflected downward from the bottom of the wing produces an upward force, and these two forces taken together lift the wing against gravity. During swimming, the hand and forearm act as the "wing," shaping the flow of water in and around the hand to optimize lift. Here are a few tips on shaping the angle of attack of the arm and hand during the catch phase of the stroke through when the hand exits the water again:

1. After the hand and arm are fully extended in the water, the wrist should flex gently down and outward, creating only a small amount of resistance against the hand. The purpose is to position the hand and forearm in nonmoving water while creating a powerful lever and setting up the lift angle.

2. Try to lead with the thumb while directing the hand downward and backward.

3. Keep the fingertips pointing nearly vertically toward the bottom of the pool until the end of the propulsion phase, just before the release and recovery begins.

4. Because the hand and forearm move diagonally as a result of body rotation, think of the stroke as a pull to the midline of the body and a push to the thigh.

Water moving backward like a current provides less resistance against the lever of the hand and arm (the propeller). In a swimming flume, hold a kickboard with your fingertips, submerge it, and pull it straight backward. There will be little resistance to the movement. In fact, the board moves quite freely. Now, hold the board at arm's length in the water, but rock or tilt the board quickly from side to side while you pull it back. If you're doing this correctly, the considerably increased resistance will prevent you from moving the kickboard at all.

The hand and forearm act in much the same way as the kickboard when you make sweeping motions during underwater movements. That is, the hand and forearm move diagonally from side to side, not straight backward. The greatest propulsive power during the underwater stroke is generated by the outward sweep. The hand is swept backward, outward, and upward, with the little finger acting as the leading edge.

Vigorously using the abdominals and hips during the upsweep phase—which is when the position of the stroking arm and axis of the body are at their most propulsive—improves speed and stroke efficiency. The chest, back, and abdominal muscles contribute substantially to the leverage and power of the stroke. This is why strengthening the core is such an important part of training, but the athlete must also learn how to recruit these muscles while swimming. To do so, as the hand begins the upsweep (as it passes from the midline of the body to the point of exit from the water), make a concentrated effort to engage the core muscles by gently compressing in the lower abdominal muscles.

This long-axis position is the essential body position taken during a world-record 800 m swim at the 1999 Pan American Games. The hips are vertically positioned at the catch as they streamline and set up the larger muscles. Swimming on the sides (along the long axis) streamlines the body so it slips through the water, reducing the number of strokes. That, of course, is your goal—to take fewer, longer, and stronger strokes.

A final important stroke tip and perhaps the most significant: Making the transition between each stroke is best achieved by keeping the underwater stroking arm in front of you until the recovery arm is even with your shoulder or just passing your head before entering the water (figure 2.6). Having your hand out in front like this, using what's called a catch-up stroke, improves the catch of the stroking arm and, most importantly, keeps the pulling hand in a position for maximum propulsion. You must not begin the stroke too early after extension, because doing so reduces momentum, glide, and most important, the functional athletic position. By positioning the stroking arm rather than "pulling" with it, the swimmer will engage the water from the most efficient, athletic, and balanced position.

Figure 2.6 The catch-up stroke.

Drills for Improving Technique

Swimming drills are used not only to teach new or poor swimmers to swim better, but also to help experienced swimmers improve their stroke control, body balance, and precision stroke movements. Most workouts should include some drills to sensitize you to improving your stroke mechanics. Keep the following points in mind when you do drills:

- Control the movement and understand the benefits and mechanics of the drill.
- Try to achieve the greatest swimming distance with each stroke.
- Use the core muscles vigorously during underwater strokes by lightly compressing the lower abdominal muscles.
- Pay particular attention to the crosswise motion of the underwater hand movements.
- Accelerate the hand during the stroke while you engage the core muscles by slightly contracting the lower abdominals.

- Remember to kick fluidly at *all* times, from start to finish, of the drill sequence. Keep the ankles loose and moving as if they are gently "boiling" the water. While many distance swimmers alternate between two-, four-, and six-beat kicks throughout an event, most triathletes think the two-beat is the only kick they need to use. I disagree and recommend that they use a six-beat kick for a few reasons. First, body balance is enhanced with a continuous, fluid kick creating constant momentum and symmetrical timing from stroke to stroke. Second, a six-beat kick is more versatile; if a triathlete knows it, he can easily change to a two- or four-beat kick to save energy if necessary. Last, the six-beat kick helps increase streamlining by reducing the amount of water over the legs, thereby reducing drag.
- Perform swim drills before the main set to maximize neurological movement and patterning.
- Occasionally time the drill sets on a short rest (a 10-second sendoff time interval). For example, if it takes 40 seconds to complete a 50 m drill, leave on a 50-second sendoff.
- Perform a test set of 8 × 50 meters of a drill every month, keeping a record of the swim time for the set (see chapter 7 for more on test sets).

ONE-ARM FREESTYLE

When performing each of the following methods, accentuate your use of the leading edge of the hand and accelerate using the core muscles, such as the abdominals and the latissimus dorsi muscles of the upper back.

One Extended, One Stroking

Trains torso rotation by developing core coordination and muscular action in this area of the body.

1. Keep your left arm extended in front of you while your right arm performs single-armed strokes over the length of the pool.
2. Focus on correctly executing the recovery, entry, extension, catch, upsweep, outsweep, and release phases.
3. Repeat with the opposite arm.

Three Left, Three Right

Trains the core and torso and facilitates neuromuscular coordination, a high elbow underwater stroke, and crosswise hand sweeping.

1. Make three complete strokes with the left arm while extending your right arm to the front.
2. Then repeat, with the right arm making the strokes while the left arm is extended.

Double-Armed Accelerators

Trains torso and core strength and coordination of release to recovery.

1. Take two left-arm followed by two right-arm strokes.
2. Emphasize core strength and hand acceleration to a full stroke.
3. Keep the kick constant during the entire stroke cycle.

THREE-TOUCH AND ENTRY GLIDE

Develops body balance, stroke coordination, glide, recovery, and kick.

1. Push off from the wall in a streamlined position, with your hands out front and your head tucked between your shoulders.
2. Take a stroke with your right arm and touch your thigh with the side of your thumb, but do not make a full extension.
3. Keep your elbow flexed (high elbow, low hand) for recovery and then bring your hand up to touch your armpit.
4. Continue the movement, bringing your hand up to touch your other, extended hand as you roll and glide onto your side with your belly facing the side of the pool.
5. Repeat with the other arm and then continue to swim down the pool, alternating arms.

Head-Up Sighting

Excellent for practicing open-water sighting; also assists in kick and underwater stroke propulsion training.

1. While your right or left arm recovers near your face, take a breath and keep your eyes above the waterline as you look ahead of you for two to four full underwater strokes.
2. Another option is to swim for one length of the pool with your head up and the water up to your chin. Or, during a distance set, swim with your head up for two or three strokes in the middle of the length.

HEAD-UP, HEAD-DOWN KICK

Helps the swimmer find her "balance point" in the water and work the hips' flexor and the upper thighs' kicking muscles. The balance point is the position in which the swimmer is most horizontal in the water and the backs of the legs and hips are riding high. Follow this drill with a 25 to 100 m swim to reinforce the neuromuscular patterning.

1. Push off from the wall in a streamlined position.
2. Without a kickboard, kick freestyle with your hands extended to the front and your ears between your shoulders.
3. Slowly lift your head until your chin is on the water's surface. Kick six times.
4. Return to the streamlined position and note the position of your hips in the water and the speed of the kick.

90-DEGREE SIDE-KICK DRILL

Teaches triathletes how to maintain stability on their sides by "gripping" the water once they move onto their sides. Improves kick mechanics and recovery coordination and body balance.

1. Push off from the wall at which you begin and end the drill. From the wall to the flag, keep the body in its streamlined, arrowlike position—hands together, arms straight, shoulders covering the ears—and use a tapered kick.

2. Stroke onto your right side (so your chin touches your right shoulder) by sweeping your left hand and forearm in toward your chest and across your abdomen. Fully extend your right hand and arm (you should be able to see the tip of your elbow) with your thumb rotated internally (tilted about 5 degrees downward).

3. Keep your left hand on your left hip.

4. Gently kick throughout the drill. At no time during this drill should the kick *not* be moving (boiling). Kick for several seconds with the leg on the side that is maintaining the chin-to-shoulder position.

5. Next, bring up your left hand, keeping your arm straight until your hand is vertical above your shoulder.

6. Return your left hand to your hip and repeat on the other side.

90-DEGREE SALUTE-ENTRY DRILL

Excellent drill for developing body balance, recovery coordination, kick mechanics, and, perhaps most important, the entry phase.

1. Push off the wall to the first flag in a streamlined position (with your ears between your shoulders and your hands together out front).

2. Slowly raise your right arm to 90 degrees and hold for one or two seconds.

3. Then, bending your elbow, lower your forearm and hand and touch the side of your forehead with the back of your hand. Hold for a second.

4. Place your fingertips in the water and then follow them with your wrist, elbow, and shoulder to complete the entry.

SIDE KICK AND ROLL

Improves the six-beat kick, coordination, hip and core rotation, and elongation of the stroke on its axis.

1. Push off from the wall in a streamlined position and execute a one-armed underwater stroke to roll onto your right side with your belly facing the side of the pool. Keep one hip at the surface of the water.
2. Now, kick-glide for six kicks in this extension-phase position.
3. Then switch to your other arm and repeat the six kicks.

Better Swimming Stretches

Before doing any stretches, warm up for 5 to 10 minutes. This warm-up may include light jogging, spinning on a stationary bike, or even light swimming to increase heart rate, blood flow, and muscle temperature.

Warming up first helps you get the most out of each stretch and reduces injury. The stretches that follow are particularly well suited for increasing your range of motion for swimming movements.

POSTERIOR CAPSULE STRETCH

Stretches the usually tight posterior and inferior joint capsules and increases shoulder internal rotation.

1. While standing, bend both arms at the elbow so that they are at chest height in front of you.
2. Close your fists with your palms facing you.
3. Place your right elbow on the joint of your left elbow.
4. Intertwine your arms and clasp your hands together.
5. Pull your left arm toward your left shoulder by moving your elbows upward and forward. This action stretches the capsule.
6. You can also perform an optional stretch of the rhomboids (the muscles in the upper back) by starting at position 2. With both arms at the center, push your elbows away from your chest and hold.

INFERIOR CAPSULE STRETCH

Improves shoulder abduction and external shoulder mobility.

1. Raise your right arm overhead.
2. Flex the elbow and put your hand on your spine.
3. Put your left arm behind your back and, without raising it, grasp the fingers of your right hand.
4. Slowly pull downward.
5. Repeat with the left arm.

ANTERIOR SHOULDER AND BICEPS STRETCH

Stretches the anterior shoulder and biceps brachii. The anterior (front) shoulder is stressed repeatedly during swimming, particularly during the underwater stroke, and the biceps flexes the forearm during the downsweep and insweep.

1. With your back facing a table, squat down placing palms down.
2. Slowly squat down further sliding your arms backward until you feel the stretch in your biceps.
3. Maintain good posture and do not lean forward.

CHEST STRETCH

Increases the length of the chest muscles, which in turn improves the range of motion of elbow and shoulder extension.

1. Stand facing an open doorway.
2. Place your right hand on the wall with your elbow at shoulder height.
3. Step through the doorway with your right leg and hold the position for 30 seconds.
4. Repeat on the left side.
5. A variation is to place both hands on either side of a corner or doorway with your elbows at shoulder height and lean forward with your knees slightly bent.

LATISSIMUS DORSI STRETCH

Stretches the back muscles, which to a great degree power the swimming stroke by helping stabilize the body's position in the water. Inflexibility in the back muscles is a common cause of overuse injuries and low back pain. Pages 16 and 17 in chapter 1 provide a way to assess your flexibility in this group of muscles.

1. Sit on the floor with your legs tucked beneath you.
2. Flex forward at the waist and use your right hand to grasp a doorframe, pole, or similar fixed object.
3. Place your head and ear on your right shoulder.
4. Lean and stretch to the right and hold this position for 30 seconds.
4. Return to the starting position and repeat for the left side.

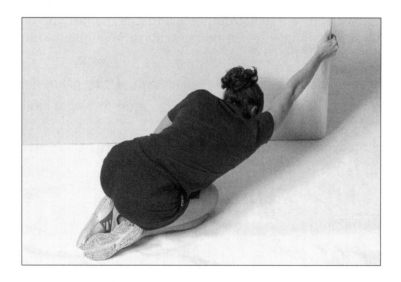

For the most part, triathletes have few choices for organized swimming workouts other than attending masters workouts. However, this is changing as the sport of triathlon continues to grow and triathlon clubs organize their own triathlete-geared swim workouts. Because triathletes' and swimmers' workouts differ in their content, this development is a good one.

Swimming with a group in an already organized program has many benefits for triathletes, as well as some disadvantages. After your swimming skills are assessed, you can decide how best to use an organized swimming program; for example, you may concentrate primarily on skill work, endurance training, interval repeats, or something else. Many programs post their workouts at the pool so you can choose the ones that make the most sense for you.

POTENTIAL BENEFITS

- Camaraderie with a group during organized workouts
- Experience of swimming alongside other swimmers
- Ability to work on drafting the swimmer in front of you (with permission, of course)
- Opportunity to participate in distance swim tests at the frequent swim meets
- Opportunity to work on non-freestyle strokes to develop your neuromuscular coordination, core strength, and feel for the water
- Access to long-course (50 m) pools, which are excellent for distance training
- Participation in structured interval and time-based workouts
- Opportunity to improve your stroke by swimming with skilled swimmers (I call this the "mimic" effect)
- Regularity of workouts
- Exposure to enthusiastic and motivating masters swim coaches

POTENTIAL DISADVANTAGES

- Possibility that workouts will not be in sync with your training periodization plan (see part II); however, many swim programs publish their workout plans well in advance of practices so you can see how they fit into your training plan and can adapt either your plan or your participation in the masters plan accordingly
- Infrequent opportunities to work on individual stroke training
- Probability that rest intervals will be too long and the distances to swim too short; most practices have few overdistance continuous swims longer than 1,500 m
- Opportunities to work on drafting are infrequent or nonexistent

Race-Ready Swim Preparation

Improving your performance in any sport requires a lot of effort, and swimming is no different. Triathletes should participate in both pool and open-water swimming events to improve their speed and efficiency and gain experience in swimming in different situations and environments. In particular, the triathlete should train frequently in open water to enhance the skills that will be used during a race. The following sections discuss several key aspects of open-water swimming, including choosing equipment, warming up, positioning at the start, drafting, sighting the course, rounding buoys, and breathing efficiently.

Choosing Equipment: Goggles, Caps, and Wetsuits

I've worn the same brand of goggles for over 20 years. At one time, another manufacturer took over the fabrication, and when I put them on, I knew immediately that something was different about the goggles. Everyone said they were identical to the older pairs, but they just didn't feel the same. Sure enough, I ultimately discovered a difference in the width of the seal. Fortunately, the old manufacturer began making the goggles again. I bought several dozen pairs.

The point of this story is that there aren't many things more important than finding goggles that fit snugly, permit clear vision, and perform to the expected standards in various environmental conditions. Putting goggles on over your swim cap, so that the goggle strap is outside, is fine for most conditions, but for heavy surf, put your goggles on first so your cap keeps the goggles from being displaced or swept away.

Wear a bright cap while swimming in open water to help protect yourself from being run over by a windsurfer, boat, or other vessel. For cold swims, when developing hypothermia is a possibility, wearing one or even two caps can make the difference between completing the swim and succumbing to the cold. If you're sensitive to cold water, you can wear a neoprene cap under a bright latex cap.

Dean Harper was one of the first triathletes to use a wetsuit in competition. Dean began racing in the early 1980s, placed among the top 10 at the Ironman Triathlon in Hawaii a couple of times, and was ranked as one of the top five triathletes in the world for long-distance events. If Mark Allen, Scott Tinley, Dave Scott, and Scott Molina were the "Big Four" in the 1980s, Dean rounded out the "Big Five." I've coached both Harper and Tinley.

Although it is possible to swim in cold water without a wetsuit—and many English Channel swimmers deride the use of wetsuits—triathlon is different from swimming. Most triathletes have a body fat level lower than that of the majority of distance open-water swimmers, so using a wetsuit in especially cold water makes sense. However, many of us old-timers have completed many triathlons without wetsuits, and I am pleased that most triathlon federations disallow the use of wetsuits when the water temperature is above 84 degrees Fahrenheit.

The wetsuit has changed the sport by increasing the number of participants. Many of these triathletes otherwise would not compete because they could not swim from, for example, Alcatraz to San Francisco in the 50-degree water of the San Francisco Bay without the insulation and flotation provided by the wetsuit. Although I agree with the argument that wetsuit-permitting events are a different challenge, I can see the overall benefit of permitting their use in colder-water events.

Technological advances resulting in the thinner fabrics of today's suits are continually reducing their impact on stroke restriction and swimming mechanics. In fact, research suggests that these newer wetsuits, often called "speed suits," are just plain fast. The speeds of intermediate-level swimmers are improved the most by a wetsuit. Swimmers of other levels of ability tend to reap benefits relating to economy rather than speed.

Warming Up

The pre-event swim warm-up often is performed incorrectly, overlooked, or avoided altogether. There is no question that a warm muscle is better suited for performance than a cold one, so it makes sense to warm up both in and out of the water, regardless of the water temperature. Doing so will not only get your heart rate up and your blood circulating, it will also warm the muscles that you will use as soon as you enter the water during the race. The length of the warm-up will depend on your swimming background and training condition and the temperature and conditions of the water.

For the experienced triathlete, a five-minute warm-up in the water may be enough along with some stretching on dry land. A neophyte triathlete with a limited swimming background should warm up in the water as well, but more as a way to acclimatize to the water than to warm the muscles; the race swim itself will be more aerobic for the beginner than for the experienced competitor, so the warm-up must not tire the triathlete before the race starts. In very cold, windy, or high-surf conditions, warming up may not be beneficial for the uninitiated because the race will likely be delayed, plus you can learn a lot by watching others navigate through the water. For example, seeing other swimmers competently negotiating the breakers by going under the wave instead of over easily demonstrates how this is the best method. In cold water situations swimming stretches explained later in this chapter are an excellent choice, along with jogging, doing calisthenics, or using elastic exercise bands to mimic swimming strokes.

Practicing Beach Starts

At the start of the race, positioning is important. Don't wait until race day to practice your group start. Get together with triathlete friends and work on compactly spaced swim starts. This can be done in open water from a beach start (preferable if this is the type of start you are preparing for) or in a 50 m pool. Just be sure that everyone gets a chance to start in the middle and stays as close to one another as possible. The goal is not to avoid congestion, but to learn how to swim in it. You can work starts into the end of any swim practice, and your confidence will increase as you gain experience in sustaining your space in close quarters. My triathletes practice this in our swim flume on a regular basis. Practice and experience teach triathletes of any level the best way to accomplish a successful start (figure 2.7).

The run up to a beach start should be practiced for ocean and lake swims. It is also a good idea to walk or jog into the water from the starting area on race day, or at least to watch others doing that so you'll be aware of any "pits" in the sand. A pit hidden in a few inches of water can send even the best triathlete tumbling into an unexpected, sandy face plant.

Do not sprint to the water, but rather gather running speed as you slowly enter the water. Raise your knees some, but not so high that you step into the water in a high knee skip style. When the water is just below your knee cap, make a diving entry into the water with both of your hands in the streamlined position out front and your ears between your shoulders, kicking and making the first strokes.

Once triathletes enter the water, they go from a vertical (running) to a horizontal (swimming) position. This changes the sizes of the gaps between competitors, making space notably tighter as the swim starts. The actions of the waves will buffet you and the other swimmers, causing you to be bumped by their arms, legs, hips, and even an occasional foot in your goggle.

© Sporting Pictures UK

Figure 2.7 Congestion during swim start.

Approach the water focusing on getting through the breakers by swimming *over* the small waves closest to the shore and *under* the crests of the breaking waves farther out. If you know this will be difficult for you, practice before the race with a group of friends or club members. You can run and walk through waves as long as they aren't more than halfway up your hip. Once waves are at that height, it is better to begin swimming to meet the next wave, which will likely be a bit larger. If you are still walking and the wave is at abdomen level or above, stand sideways to the wave. This presents less body surface and reduces the amount of distance you may be pushed back. Now, you must begin to swim to meet the next wave. If the wave is breaking, dip under the wave just as it approaches by taking a breath of air and submerging yourself just below the base of the wave. If you're swimming as a wave approaches (which is best), swim under the crest of the wave by stroking into the wave and holding both arms outstretched in front. In a moment the wave will pass and you'll be swimming down the back side of the wave. Repeat this until you've swum past the breakers and are in the swells. Remember, stay relaxed and stretch out your stroke "long and loose" so you don't go into oxygen debt.

Beginning the Swim

For the strong swimmer, starting up front is essential, even if you feel you're two or three seconds per 100 m slower than the best swimmer. As faster swimmers move by, stay close alongside them and then tuck in behind. Strong swimmers surpassing slower swimmers must be considerate and refrain from literally swimming over the others, as has happened too many times. Such behavior isn't good sportsmanship, so don't do it!

The intermediate swimmer is presented with more challenges than swimmers of other skill levels because the majority of competitors are in this class. In a densely packed area, your swimming style must be more give-and-take because normal mechanics are all but lost. Specifically, your arms' out-of-water recovery, entry, and release may be obstructed by other swimmers, so much of what you've learned and drilled in the pool will be more difficult to execute. This is why being able to substitute one out-of-water recovery technique for another, learning to breathe equally well on both sides (bilateral breathing), and training to gain experience in swimming in congestion are important.

Novice and recreational swimmers have several choices for starting an open-water ocean or lake swim. Most choose to start at the back of the pack, far to one side, or to wait until the coast is clear of other swimmers. I discourage the use of all of these tactics because they add time and distance and are tantamount to dodging the swim instead of fully participating in it. Instead, these swimmers should start in the middle. The faster swimmers will quickly pull away, the turmoil will last only a minute or so, and as your swimming improves—and it will—you'll learn to swim in these conditions.

One of the best open-water swimmers I've coached is John Aver. John is not a good pool swimmer; in fact, others can swim much faster than he can in a pool. Put John in the ocean or a lake, however, and he becomes one of the best in an amazing transformation. John attributes his excellent open-water performance to his focusing on "hunting feet" throughout the swim. If another swimmer is anywhere near him, John drafts, or swims right behind, him to take advantage of the lower water pressure there.

Swimming Beyond the Breakers

Here, the open water often becomes a magnificent, elegant place to swim. If the swells aren't too big and it isn't too windy, the waves will gently buoy you up and down—a very pleasant experience. Otherwise, wave patterns can be so choppy that you feel like you're in a washing machine stuck in the agitation cycle.

In windy, choppy, and crowded conditions, having the ability to switch between the high elbow, low hand recovery and the low elbow, high hand recovery is important. The more streamlined the swimmer's stroke is and the less impeded it is by the strokes of others, the easier it is to alternate between the two. Therefore, it is vital that when wave action or narrow swimming lanes impede movement, the swimmer feels comfortable changing the recovery motion.

The priority then becomes sighting and swimming the shortest possible course that lies within your capabilities. Remain calm, keep your perceived exertion at a moderate level, and focus on staying relaxed, breathing smoothly with every stroke, and occasionally sighting your course.

A triathlete can use strokes other than the freestyle during competition. In addition, practicing backstroke, breaststroke, and butterfly swimming can help you develop better freestyle mechanics because from a neuromuscular standpoint, each of these strokes challenges the mind and body to coordinate themselves for more efficient movement. Perhaps most important, all of these strokes teach hand-sculling patterns that can be used in freestyle swimming.

In open-water swimming, being able to switch to another stroke proficiently is advantageous for a number of reasons, as some of the best open-water swimmers know. Moving from freestyle to backstroke—an almost effortless movement—allows you to see what's behind you, rest, or navigate between two points. Changing to breaststroke after rounding a buoy lets you check landmarks and possibly even catch a draft, since everyone rounding the buoy is swimming at about the same speed. It makes sense to save energy at this time.

Learning to Draft

Drafting is a technique used not so much in competitive pool swimming (since each swimmer has her own lane in a race), but it's frequently performed in open-water swimming competitions. Swimmers who actively avoid drafting wind up swimming farther to steer clear of other competitors. When you're swimming with 50, 100, 200, or 1,000 or more swimmers, drafting is simply part of the game that can't be avoided. Plus, swimmers benefit by following in the wake of others' feet or swimming alongside another individual or group of swimmers: Drafting increases speed, reduces energy costs, and improves the navigation of some competitors.

I teach all of my athletes to draft. Triathlon and open-water swims are frenzied, and the sooner an athlete accepts this, the better her swimming performance becomes. In addition, there's nothing like experiencing the unsettled dynamics of interacting with 200 or so flapping arms and legs and the elements.

There are several methods of drafting in open water. The most common is to swim directly behind a sole swimmer or a group. Each time your arm enters the water, move as close as possible to the feet of the swimmers you're drafting on. From time to time, you'll touch their feet. Don't slap the feet in stroke after stroke—you'll only stir the ire of your competitor and wind up eating his heel when he executes a series of kick propulsions to teach you a lesson. Try to be courteous, but know that occasionally touching the feet of the person in front of you (or having your feet touched by the person behind you) is just as much a part of the game as wearing a wetsuit is nowadays.

How do you know if you're drafting optimally behind the right person or group of swimmers? If you see the white bubbles formed by the feet in front of you, you're hydroplaning, and you aren't losing contact or being lifted (hips up) by the wake, you are in the right position. You should not feel as though you are exerting with your maximum intensity, but it should not be easy, either. When drafting, you must remain alert and work reasonably hard to maintain contact. Just keep following and don't look up too often—let them lead or be led.

Sighting While Breathing

Part of good sighting is knowing the course *before* the start. It is not so important to know where the buoys are, but know their positional relationships to higher landmarks—landmarks that you'll be able to see when you're in the water with several hundred other swimmers. Use these landmarks instead of the buoys when you swim away from, alongside, or toward the shore. Then, look for the buoy when you're 100 to 200 yards away. Waves, sun, troughs, crests, and other swimmers' splashes and arms can hide the buoy, but a land feature, bridge, pier, anchored boat, or other large object can keep you on course (figure 2.8).

Keep in mind that the higher and more often you lift your head to sight the course, the more energy and time it will take you to swim it. Instead, sight by using this more efficient method: As you are about to take a breath, bring up your chin and "peek" just before you turn your head to the side to take the breath. You can do this several times in a row without increasing your drag by dropping your hip, which costs energy.

Don't wait until race day to practice sighting. In fact, frequently do "head up" swimming while training. Every so often during a swim set—even the harder ones—lift your chin, sight, and breathe. Over time you'll improve.

Breathing on both sides is another open-water swimming skill that must be practiced and perfected. The skilled swimmer can breathe comfortably on either side without losing speed or efficiency. In training, try breathing on every third stroke during most swims and breathing on just the weak side during swims of varying types and intensities. This will not only help your open-water swimming, it will also stabilize your stroke bilaterally, thereby improving your underwater efficacy.

© Sporting Pictures UK

Figure 2.8 Sighting during an open-water swim.

Keeping Your Composure

At one time or another, every open-water swimmer is challenged by a fearful situation. Of course, just about every time you ride your bike or run, you are faced with equally fearful circumstances (cars, mainly). But many people fear unknown creatures, tidal waves, and other mysteries of the sea, causing them trepidation when swimming in open water.

We need to have a healthy respect for the oceans and lakes we use. The water is going to win a fight every time, and struggling is the quickest way to get into difficulty. Try to be in concert with the water as you move through it; become part of it by streamlining yourself and maintain your composure by concentrating on sighting, rounding the buoys, and pacing yourself with long and relaxed strokes. With practice, you'll find yourself gaining skill and confidence in swimming in the open water.

Few circumstances engender the quietude of open-water swimming in a glassy-smooth lake on a cool summer morning in the mountains. Few, too, are as disquieting as being 1 of 500 swimmers flickering through the water toward the rising sun. Remember that competition in a triathlon's open-water swimming event is like the movement of a flock of birds. There's a leader and there are followers. If everyone follows the leader, they swim the same course. So, although being part of the chaos may be a little uncomfortable, it does have benefits. Accepting and being part of the turmoil can even be fun, and it prevents you from swimming a longer and slower course by looking for clear water.

Exiting the Water

If there are breakers, swimmers need to learn how to "bodysurf" the waves as they approach the shore. Catching waves requires good timing, additional kicking, and sometimes even sprinting, depending on the size of the wave. When the wave approaches and is about to break, try to get on top of the wave and hold both arms out in front of you with your fists closed. As the wave starts to break with white water, start swimming again, attempting to stay on top of the wave.

CHAPTER 3

Pure Cycling

The cycling phase of triathlon is a very interesting aspect of the sport whether the race is being conducted as a customary nondrafting race; an Olympic, draft-legal race; or a modern criterium (lap) race used by professional triathletes.

There are huge differences between a competitive road cyclist and a triathlete in terms of the techniques used, body position on the bike, and bike-handling skill. Comparing them is difficult in many ways, but some of the fundamentals are similar, and analyzing these similarities and differences is the pathway by which we can determine how a triathlete can best ride the cycling portion of the event.

Cycling is much more than just pushing on the pedals. Each triathlete has a unique relationship with her bicycle that is based on fit, technique, gearing, and speed. As with swimming and running, good technique, strength, flexibility, and body position are important elements in overall performance. However, cycling adds to the mix the bike and its components. The way the rider interacts with the bicycle due to the frame size and shape, the wheels, tire type and inflation, positioning, crank length, and other variables affects efficiency. Additional factors like wind, hilly terrain, friction, heat, cold, on-bike nutritional intake, and altitude increase the challenges of proficient riding.

Body Position and Bike Fitting

Efficiency or economy of movement is often measured as the amount of energy or number of calories expended to complete a given task; how much energy is spent depends in large part on the effectiveness of the rider's technique, as we have already discussed in relationship to swimming and will shortly consider on the bike. In cycling, the triathlete faces numerous decisions that affect performance—aerodynamics and drag, body position, pedaling biomechanics, and bike components. In this section, we look at the most important of these points, body positioning and bike fit. If all of the best equipment in the world is carrying you but the biomechanical power is inefficiently distributed to the pedals, then it truly isn't about the bike.

The starting point for improving any bicycling technique is ensuring that you are fitted properly to your machine. Any musculoskeletal, endurance, strength, and flexibility improvements you make will directly affect your fit on the bike. Because bike fitting is a dynamic process—that is, adjustments are necessary because training cycles, seasons, fitness, climate, flexibility, and events vary—we review how you can check your fit on the bike yourself by setting up your bike on an indoor trainer and having a coach or friend take some measurements while you position yourself on the bike. You'll need some basic bike tools, a goniometer to measure angles (I like the long-armed models), and a level with a string with a weight attached to use as a plumb line. I currently assess bike fit using a combination of measurements of hip, knee, shoulder, and elbow angles and a CompuTrainer (Pro model 3D). The CompuTrainer ergometer (www.computrainer.com), which has SpinScan, watt, and torque features, allows you to dial in the fit.

It's important to spend time measuring your body's angles on the bike to achieve the most comfortable and efficient fit. Bike positioning is "dynamic," and fit should be assessed several times a year for best results. The cost of a professional fitting can range from $250 to $700 or more, depending on the services chosen. If injury has been a recurrent problem and you have tried fitting yourself, a professional bike fitting may be worth the extra expense; for most triathletes, however, this is not an option. Using the following procedures should help you get a good bike fit on your own.

Saddle Height

Saddle height is central to achieving the optimal bike fit, body position, and production of muscle force. The amount of extension and flexion of the knee during the pedal stroke is determined by the height of the saddle, the position of the cleat to the pedal axle, and the position of the saddle along the top tube.

1. Make certain the ball of your foot is positioned directly over or slightly behind the pedal axle. To do this, you may need to adjust the position of the cleat on the bottom of the shoe.

2. Position the crank arm at the bottom—dead center—and place a marker on the floor directly under the crank arm.

3. Get on the bike and spin for a few minutes in the aero position. Do not slide forward on the saddle.

4. Gradually reduce your cadence and come to a slow stop over the marker. Your foot will be at the bottom of the stroke.

5. Have a friend place a goniometer on the trochanter to measure the angle lateral to the knee. I like to place a level on the vertical arm of the goniometer to ensure that the measurement is accurate.

6. The angle from your hip to your knee should be between 25 and 32 degrees—28 degrees is optimal (figure 3.1a).

7. Adjust the saddle until the hip–knee angle is within this range. To achieve the right angle, raise the seat post if the angle is less than 26 degrees and lower it if it is more than 32.

Saddle Position

This test will confirm if the saddle is too far back or forward.

1. Place your foot on the pedal at the 3 o'clock position.

2. Move your knee inward so it touches the top tube.

3. Drop a plumb line from the front of your kneecap.

4. The plumb should pass through the center of the axle. If it is either forward of or behind this, move the saddle to line it up (figure 3.1b).

5. If you move the saddle, recheck its height to make sure the 28-degree angle has been maintained.

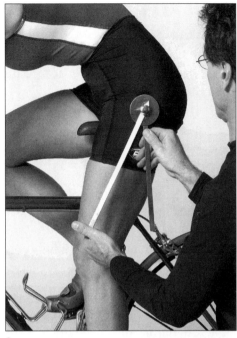

a

b

Figure 3.1, a-b   Saddle height measurement (*a*); saddle position measurement (*b*).

Elbow and Shoulder Angle

1. While you are positioned on the aero bars, have your partner place the goniometer at the side of your shoulder.
2. Swing the goniometer arm to the lateral bony point of your elbow (the epicondyle).
3. This angle should be the same as that of the hip and knee (between 26 and 32 degrees). If it isn't, either your stem is too short or long or your saddle is too far forward or back.

Stem Height

1. Measure the height of the stem from the ground to its topmost point and the height of the saddle from the ground to its tip (forward-most point).
2. The difference in height between the saddle and the stem ideally should be 2.5 centimeters, and no more than 5 centimeters.

Aero Bar Angle

The goal of setting up the aero bars correctly is to streamline the body into an aerodynamic and mechanically sound position.

1. Measure the angle of the bars in relation to the top tube by placing the goniometer on the top tube and adjusting the measuring arm to determine the angle.
2. In general, the angle of the bars in relation to the top tube is between 18 and 28 degrees, but because your comfort is fundamentally important, a range of adjustments is acceptable (figure 3.1c). Positioning the

Figure 3.1c   Aero-bar angle.

angle appropriately places the body in a more functional and athletic posture. Too low or too high an angle leaves the triathlete unbalanced and less effectively positioned to transmit power to the pedals.

3. Position the bars to reduce airflow onto your torso by adjusting the angle so the back is relatively flat. Too low and the back rounds by flexing and too high, the back will arch.

4. Keep the elbow pads narrow so your knees are hidden by your elbows and the airflow is streamlined.

The Athletic Posture and Performance

As described in chapter 1, an athletic posture is one that is stable and functional. The back is straight, the chest is up, and the ears are in alignment with the shoulders whether the athlete is swimming, riding, or running. Just look at Lance Armstrong climbing to see what I mean (figure 3.2). Athletes who maintain this posture are likely to perform better by improving speed and stamina, increasing muscular power, and lessening the risk of musculoskeletal overuse injury. In effect, the athlete uses a larger cross section of specific cycling muscles instead of smaller ancillary muscles that don't contribute as efficiently to optimal performance.

© Empics

Figure 3.2 Lance Armstrong (far right) demonstrates perfect posture.

This athletic posture is a position almost every triathlete can achieve. However, there are limitations of muscle length and strength that may hinder the perfect riding position. Triathletes come in all shapes and sizes, so it's impossible to pattern every rider in the same exact position; fitting the bike to the rider becomes a process of trial and error involving first assessing muscle lengths and strengths and then improving them (chapter 1) to help to attain a more functional riding position.

The goal of the flexibility and strength training I put into every athlete's program is to ultimately improve performance, but the underlying focus is on maintaining a sound musculoskeletal system to prevent overuse injuries. Knee pain (anterior and lateral) is perhaps the most common complaint from cycling. Sources of this type of overuse are errors in training periodization (too much and too intense training), body posture relating to the saddle position (its height and distance downward, forward, and backward), cleat position, gearing, and cadence, as well as flexibility restrictions and muscular imbalances.

Posture problems that position the rider's head, neck, and shoulders incorrectly over the aero bars often cause neck and back pain for the triathlete. However, faulty workplace ergonomics and poor sitting and standing body posture may also contribute to a weakening of the core stabilizing muscles of the abdominals, hips, and, back. If these muscles are weak, supporting the correct posture on the bike will be difficult for them and lead to pain. Again, this is where dryland conditioning exercises can help by strengthening and lengthening these core muscles.

Watching a world-class cyclist climb gives you a good idea of how much more efficient the correct cycling posture can be compared to a less-stable position on the bike. There was no better example of this than during the 2001 Tour de France climb of L'Alpe d'Huez. At the bottom of the 21-kilometer climb, Lance Armstrong grimaced in pain and slouched over his frame, feigning suffering to make his opponents and the commentators believe he was out of the race for the day.

Just after the television showed a wavering Armstrong, he moved to the front of the peloton, took one last look back at rival Jan Ullrich, and convincingly pulled away to charge up the mountain and win a memorable stage by just under two minutes. The win was impressive, but more impressive to me was his carriage on the bike as he climbed. There was a distinct difference between his posture on the bike and that of his other world-class competitors.

I remember immediately commenting that Armstrong's body position on that climb was unmistakably more functional than that of the other riders. The key points of Armstrong's climbing position are the following:

- His back is straight and upright throughout the climb.
- His ears align with his shoulders (head up).
- His chest is elevated.

- At the bottom of the downstroke his leg does *not* straighten.
- There is little sideways motion as his hips and thighs work as a functional unit.

One can easily see the differences between a less-effective posture and Armstrong's highly functional posture in replays of the climb. Armstrong's competitors' positions did not fully use their core muscles to their advantage—their heads dropped, their bodies sagged, and their performance declined.

In contrast, Armstrong's position took full advantage of his core. An athlete at any level can train himself to maintain this functional athletic position when climbing, descending, and on the flats. Maintain a straight back and tall chest and begin pedal movements from the core.

Better Cycling Technique

Learning to ride as efficiently as possible is more than clipping in and just turning the cranks around and around. To become fluid and smooth on the bike, a triathlete needs to learn and drill with specific pedaling motions—the downstroke, backstroke, upstroke, and overstroke.

In its simplest form, an optimal pedaling stroke generates more torque during the downstroke. The efficient pedaling stroke does not push and pull, but rather has an elliptical (oval) motion. To see this for yourself, find a long and gentle uphill slope. As you pedal, note how your foot tends to emphasize the downstroke, pull backward slightly on the backstroke, briefly and almost unnoticeably pull on the upstroke, and press into the overstroke.

Essentially, learning pedaling mechanics is about learning to recruit the appropriate muscles during the right time of the stroke. During each sector of the pedal stroke, the hip flexors, quadriceps, hamstrings, gastrocnemius, and gluteus muscles load and unload within changing continuums of force. Many triathletes demonstrate poor energy transference, a throbbing, uneven, and unproductive stroke. What you see in experienced riders, on the other hand, is an increased ability to recruit muscles, resulting in seemingly effortless pedaling action.

The backstroke, upstroke, and overstroke are what I call the transitional phases of the pedal stroke. They do not provide a noticeable amount of total power, but they transition from and to the downstroke, which provides 97 percent or more of the total watts during a stroke.

The foot and pedal move elliptically, but the force applied to the pedal varies throughout the 360 degrees of the stroke. The position of the foot (heel up or down) also varies with the ankling preferences of the rider. Ankling, a technique used during the pedaling stroke, is characterized by the flexion (heel up) and extension (heel down) of the foot while pedaling.

The chief goal of pedaling is to limit the amount of deceleration of momentum. Therefore, maintaining an evenly paced and circular momentum to the cranks results in what we see as a fluid and efficient stroke.

Downstroke: The downstroke begins as the foot and pedal move from 0 to 180 degrees, with the largest thrust generated between 45 and 135 degrees (figure 3.3). The motion of the foot is directed by pushing the ball of the foot forward and downward. Some cyclists push the heel down slightly below the axle of the pedal during this sector, which seems to set up the next phase, the backstroke, and promotes the stability of momentum.

Backstroke: The backstroke is the sector immediately following (and overlapping) the downstroke (figure 3.3). The backstroke transitions from the downstroke by pulling backward along the bottom of the stroke. It is important to note that the opposite leg is entering the downstroke at this time. To this end, I advise clients to make this movement smoothly and without concentrating on torque. Rather, as with each of the transitional sectors, the goal is to maintain momentum. While one leg is in a dominant torque, the other is in transition, and attempting to engage both legs simultaneously with equal thrust will only lessen the total watts generated and result in an awkward and inefficient style.

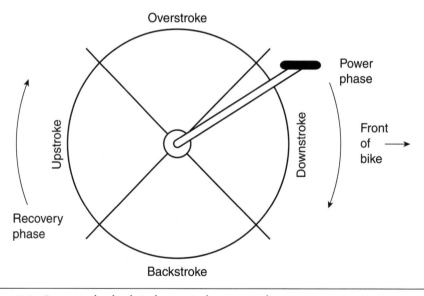

Figure 3.3 Downstroke, backstroke, upstroke, overstroke.

Upstroke: The upstroke follows the backstroke and emphasizes the continuum of momentum. For that reason, it is best if you do not exaggerate the effort, but bring up the pedal smoothly and subtly. In conditions like climbing or when the rider is out of the saddle, the power used during the upstroke can be more concentrated; pulling up can be beneficial at times, using the arms to counterbalance and pull down while pushing down and pulling up on the pedal.

Overstroke: The overstroke transitions between the upstroke and the downstroke and is accomplished by pressing the foot forward. Once more, there is only a small, perhaps unnoticeable force generated during this sector. However, this does not diminish the overstroke's importance because the goal is to maintain momentum throughout the pedaling stroke.

Shoe and Clip-On Pedal Interface

Make certain your shoe and pedal complement each other effectively by getting the closest connection between the shoe, cleat, and pedal. Adapters are available to mount different manufacturer's models of shoes to pedals. However, sometimes there is a trade-off in performance with adapters because the greater the distance between the shoe and the pedal, the lower the transfer of energy. The best way to eliminate this is to buy shoes with a firm sole material such as carbon fiber that are lightweight, fit snugly and comfortably, and match (or at least are compatible with) the pedal system.

Cycling Drills for Better Technique

The pedal stroke of accomplished triathletes and cyclists is smooth, fluid, relaxed, elliptical, and appears to be effortless. This of course is the result of many thousands of miles of distance rides, interval training, technique drilling, and racing. For triathletes, however, the challenge is to achieve efficiency while concurrently training in swimming and running.

For this reason, one of the best uses of a triathlete's time on the bike is to work on cycling technique to improve the efficacy of performance. Time trials are all about the efficient transfer of energy. A smooth pedaling stroke that is relaxed, fluid, dynamic, and effortless is essential. The position of the body is functional—aerodynamic and relaxed. The hands, shoulders, arms, and even the facial muscles are calm and maintain an effortless, stress-free pose.

The following technical-form drills have been developed over my 20 years of coaching triathletes. Drills are a cornerstone of effective training, enabling elite athletes to improve and teaching experienced, recreational, and neophyte athletes how to activate neuromuscular movements and patterning (brain to muscle response). Practice the drills as part of your warm-up, after an interval, or during a cool-down on an indoor trainer, rollers, or the road.

STANDING CORE DRILL

Strengthens the transverse abdominus muscles, which stabilize the pelvis, and increases their function as an important postural stabilizer.

1. Ride in a large gear standing out of the saddle. The duration can be from several seconds to perhaps 20 minutes and take place over flats, rolling terrain, or even climbs. The longer the interval, the less torque or pedal pressure is applied. In other words, keep the intensity moderate.

2. Contract your lower abdominal muscles throughout the interval by squeezing lightly during the entire duration of the interval.

3. While riding out of the saddle, you can perform the following exercises, as well:

   - Down-, back-, up-, and overstroke isolations (work each separately)
   - High-rpm (revolutions per minute) spinning by selecting a small gear such as 39 × 21 and riding for varying intervals
   - Press, push, and pull (press forward from the top of the stroke, push down, and then pull up with the opposite crank)

LOW-GEAR, HIGH-RPM DRILL

This drill improves recruitment, neuromuscular patterning, and pedaling technique under light gearing and faster rpm. Execute this drill on flats, hills, and rolling terrain while alternating riding seated or standing out of the saddle.

1. In a low gear (39 × 21, 19, 18), spin the pedals at high rotations in intervals lasting from 10 seconds to two minutes. Repeat two to five times.

2. Begin at 100 rpm and work up to 120 or more.

3. Make certain your hips do not rock from side to side.

HIGH-GEAR, LOW-RPM DRILL

This drill develops a strong, elliptical stroke by using low revolutions and light gearing. Execute this drill on flats, hills, and rolling terrain while alternating riding seated or standing out of the saddle.

1. In a high gear (53×13, 14, 15), spin the pedals at low rpm for intervals of one to five minutes.
2. Begin at 70 rpm and go as low as 50.

ISOLATED-LEG SPINNING

There is little doubt that one-legged spinning improves pedaling efficiency. Isolate your right side as your left leg and foot relax and apply no pressure. The result is an almost perfect spin with well over 97 percent of the total power coming during the downstroke. While you spin with the right leg only, slowly bring the left leg in "matching" the same mechanics of the right. Repeating this for both legs during a warm-up, cool-down, or even as part of high- or low-rpm intervals training can be of significant benefit to pedaling efficiency.

Descending Spins: Begin with 10 spins using the right leg and then 10 using the left. Switch back to the right leg for 9 spins, then the left for 9, then the right for 8 spins, the left for 8, and so on until you finish with 1 spin with the right and 1 with the left.

Ascending Spins: Do this drill in the same way you did the decreasing-spins drill, but start with 1 spin on each side and finish with 10 on each side.

Descending and Ascending Spins: Go from 10 spins to 1 with the right leg and then from 1 spin to 10 with the left leg. Repeat decreasing from 10 spins to 1 with the left leg and increasing from 1 to 10 spins with the right.

Sectors: Divide the pedaling stroke into four quadrants and work on each one independently. For example, you could drill for four minutes (working on the downstroke, backstroke, upstroke, and overstroke for one minute) or for one minute (spending 15 seconds on working each sector).

HIGH-RPM

High-rpm (Hrpm) drills train the pedaling motion by improving muscular movements and control and improving stroke biomechanics. On top of that, it's not bad cardiovascular training, either! The drill and the method of spinning you use is one of the best for learning and training an effective pedaling stroke and smooth spin. You'll learn to optimize stroke mechanics with fast, light, low-intensity pedaling action. The gearing is low, producing spins of 120 rpm or more. Begin and end just about every cycling workout with Hrpm spinning drills. I like for my athletes to do these on rollers or trainers, but the road is fine, too (especially on downhills, where revolutions can easily reach well over 120). Rollers (which I prefer over trainers for their help with proprioceptive training) give riders an uninterrupted exercise session with a constant workload.

The following is a combined low- and high-gear workout focusing on high revolutions. There is no break between the sets. Although the workout can be done on the road, it is designed for rollers.

> 2 minutes at 85 rpm in low gear (39/21)
>
> 3 minutes at 90 rpm in high gear (42/16)
>
> 4 minutes at 95 rpm in low gear (39/23)
>
> 3 minutes at 100 rpm in high gear (42/14)
>
> 2 minutes at 105 rpm in high gear (42/12)
>
> 3 minutes at 110 rpm in low gear (39/21)
>
> 4 minutes at 115 rpm in high gear (42/18)
>
> 2 minutes at 120 rpm in low gear (39/21)

SINGLE-LEGGED ACCELERATION

Isolated single-legged drills reduce fluctuations in pedaling power. Single-legged accelerations improve neuromuscular economy by increasing nerve stimulation. Essentially, the transferring of power to the pedals becomes more efficient because the drill enhances the forward and downward motion of the downstroke as it smoothes the backstroke, upstroke, and overstroke.

Two methods for doing this drill are with low rpm at a high gear or with high rpm at a low gear for accelerations. In the low-rpm version, the cyclist accelerates from 70 to 80 rpm in a high gear, which permits a full application of power around the 360 degrees of the pedal stroke. For the high-rpm version, accelerate from 90 to 110 rpm or more while using a light (low) gear.

> 1. Warm up each leg (left then right) for 8 × 15 seconds at high rpm and a high gear plus 30 seconds of both legs normal at a smooth spin. In

39/18 (chainring/gear), accelerate from 90 to 100 rpm 1 through 4 and 95 to 105 rpm during 5 through 8.

2. 4 × 30 seconds at low rpm and in a high gear with each leg plus 1 minute with both legs pedaling for a smooth normal spinning in a lower gear. In 42/14, accelerate from 70 to 80 rpm during each interval.

3. 12 × 15 seconds at high 100 rpm and low gear with the left leg plus 15 seconds at low 75 rpm and high gear with the right leg.

ONE-LEGGED SPINNING

This drill helps develop neuromuscular control, spin efficiency, constant stroke pressure (particularly during the downstroke and backstroke phases), and opposite-leg coordination.

Back in 1981, I often had athletes come to my back porch in Walnut Creek, California, for spinning workouts. That's what I called them back then and, with very loud music blasting from my speakers, my athletes on "turbo trainers" spun these and many of the drills in this chapter. Now, of course, this type of workout, known as "spinning," is common at health clubs.

This one-legged spin drill was one of the first that I came up with. At the time, its effectiveness could be established only theoretically, but the analytical equipment available today confirms that this is the most effective drill for improving the performance of the spin stroke. By isolating each pedaling stroke, you can enhance your brain-to-muscle coordination, especially during the downstroke. Isolating each spin teaches an athlete what a good stroke should feel like. Keep both feet in the pedals, but isolate one foot to dominate as the other simply tags along, applying no force to or pressure on the pedal.

If you want to improve cycling in more ways than just aerodynamically, pay close attention to your pedaling stroke. Pedaling involves more than just moving your legs up and down.

1. Warm up by pedaling for two minutes alternating one-legged spins at 15-second intervals.

2. Continue pedaling, alternating legs at 30-second intervals, for another four minutes.

3. 6 × 1 minute alternating legs as follows: 5 seconds alternating, 10 seconds alternating, 15 seconds alternating, 20 seconds alternating, and 2 × 30-second alternating.

4. 8 × 2 minutes. Over four periods of two minutes each, alternate legs every 30 seconds, then every 20 seconds, every 10, and every 5. Repeat.

5. Cool down for two minutes, alternating legs at 15-second intervals.

Descending and Ascending One-Legged Spinning

1. Warm up for 10 minutes by spinning in a small chainring at 95 rpm working the downstroke. Work the odd minutes in the small chainring and the even minutes below in the large chainring.
2. 4 ×10 to 1 spins. Pedal 10 spins with the right leg, then 10 with the left. Switch back to the right leg for 9 spins, then the left for 9, and so on down to 1 spin on each side. Repeat three times.
3. 4 × 1 to 10 spins. Pedal 1 spin with the right leg and 1 with the left, then 2 with the right leg and 2 with the left, and so on up to 10 with the right and 10 with the left.
4. Cool down for 10 minutes, alternating every minute between pedaling standing and seated in a small ring (39/16).

STABILITY DRILL

This drill can do a lot to help triathletes develop better balance, bike-handling skill, and confidence. It also improves tracking (sideways wheel motion) and cornering (inside knee coordination). The drill is best performed on a safe street, cul-de-sac, or corner of a parking lot.

1. Shift into your lowest gear ratio (i.e., 39/23).
2. Slowly ride in a small circle that turns to the right for two revolutions.
3. Turn out and go in the other direction for two revolutions.
4. Then, complete one circle that turns to the right and again pull out and complete a circle that turns to the left. You've just completed a figure eight.
5. Repeat steps 1 to 4, but begin with circles that turn to the left.

SECTORS DRILL

At about the same time I started using the one-legged spinning and Hrpm drills, I also began using sectors training as a means of enhancing the pedaling stroke actions and the transition from one phase to another. The intention is to lessen jerky movements in the downstroke, backstroke, upstroke, and overstroke and make the complete stroke more fluid.

1. Perform Hrpm from 95 to 105 rpm for eight minutes while applying downstroke only (both legs).
2. Complete 4 × 1 minute each of the following isolated sectors: downstroke, backstroke, upstroke, and overstroke.

3. Perform Hrpm from 100 to 110 rpm for six minutes, applying back-stroke only.

4. Complete 8 × 30 seconds of each sector.

5. Perform Hrpm from 95 to 105 rpm for four minutes, applying up-stroke only.

6. Complete 16 × 15 seconds of each sector.

7. Perform Hrpm from 100 to 110 rpm for two minutes, applying over-stroke only.

Optimizing Cadence and Gearing

Your goal is to use a cadence that enables you to most efficiently use your energy. The cadence varies for each individual depending on the length of the event and the fitness level.

Slower cadences are generally indicated for higher gear choices, which require more energy, because they decrease the length of time until fatigue. For shorter, power events, this might be a good choice. On the other hand, a higher pedaling tempo, or spinning, uses less energy and can result in faster overall times for longer events. Perhaps that is why the world's best cycling climbers tend to spin at faster rates.

Is there an optimal cadence? Essentially, there are ranges of optimum spin rates for different types of events, course profiles, levels of fitness, muscle-fiber makeup, gearing, and even environmental conditions. Cadences also vary in relation to energy stores, length of ride, wind, elevation, and terrain. Despite all of these variables, however, the variations in optimal pedaling rates are not too broad. Efficient cadences tend to be between 80 and 115 rpm. Under most conditions over flat land and rolling hills, cadences of 90 to 115 rpm are effective. For long hills, try to maintain 80 to 95 rpm.

Due to its variability, setting an exact heart rate to "lock into" isn't practical. So, too, is the case with cadence rates. The best ways to measure intensity on the bike are with ratings of perceived exertion (RPE) and pedaling pressure. Pedal pressure changes are the first indication that your cadence is either too slow or too fast and whether the gear is too easy or too hard. As pedal pressure force increases, there is a corresponding elevation of RPE. When this happens, it's time to shift to a lighter, lower gear so you can maintain a more uniform pace. When the pedal force is too light, rpm increases and RPE lessens, which sometimes indicates a need to shift into a higher (harder) gear ratio.

Experimenting while riding with other triathletes is an outstanding way to determine pedaling cadence and efficiency. The next time you're climbing with a group and find the pace difficult or are losing contact switch to a lower gear increasing the rpm somewhat. I've noted on many instances triathletes will actually "close the gap" and the RPE/HR goes down. The point being there is a "fine-line" for "fine-tuning" cadence and energy output. The triathlete during training can experiment and thereby develop the "feel" for the right cadence.

One cycling error that many triathletes are often guilty of is riding in gears that are too high, resulting in a slower cadence. That is, they tend to choose gears with a harder, higher gear ratio, which over a long ride results in slower times.

The most efficient cyclist changes gears as terrain conditions, energy use, and cadence demand (figure 3.4). Doing so preserves energy and maintains pace over a longer period. Improving gear choice is an indispensable part of learning how to ride more efficiently, so it is important to get to know your gearing! What you need to know is the shifting sequence that follows the chainring and cassette on your bike. The result of selecting the wrong gear during a race is expending too much or too little energy, thus losing time.

You can figure out the shifting sequence of your gears by using a gear chart (available at bike stores or on the web) until you are able to determine by feel which gears are most effective for the conditions of the course.

© Empics

Figure 3.4   2000 Olympic Triathlon (Sydney, Australia).

1. Separately, divide the number of teeth in your large and small chainrings by the number of teeth in each cassette cog.

2. Multiply this by your wheel diameter (inches or metric).

3. The result is the number of gear inches, which indicates the distance the wheels will travel with one rotation of the pedaling crank arm. (The results for a 9-speed cassette and 53/39 chainring would be 18 gear inches, for example.)

4. Eliminate the small chainring and smallest cog and the large ring and largest cog. The angles of these gears are too great and they increase frictional drag on the chain, resulting in grinding of the chainring.

5. Select respective gears that are about six gear inches apart. Anything greater will feel too high or too low and inadequately distribute energy to the pedals.

Improving Flexibility for Cycling

I believe flexibility to be central to athletic performance. Simply put, shortened or restricted muscles limit range of motion and thus power, which in turn reduce performance capacity. This is why the musculoskeletal assessment (chapter 1) is such an important part of my work with endurance athletes. I like to objectively determine muscle lengths before designing the program and then reassess them to monitor improvements. In just about every instance where there is a restriction in the range of motion, there is a contributing musculoskeletal injury that needs care. The following stretches are excellent for improving your cycling-specific flexibility.

STANDING QUADRICEPS

1. While standing, contract your abdominals to place your pelvis in a neutral position. Do *not* arch your back.

2. Lift your right lower leg to bring your heel close to the gluteals.

3. With your right or left hand, gently hold the ankle; your right knee should point toward the floor.

4. Press your front hipbone forward and slightly extend your hip.

5. Keep your torso lifted and your head up.

6. Repeat with the left leg.

SIDE-LYING QUADRICEPS

1. Stretch out on your left side with your head resting on your left arm.
2. Pull in the abdominals to place your pelvis in a neutral position.
3. Bend your right leg at the knee to bring your ankle back toward the gluteals.
4. Reach back with your right hand and gently hold the ankle with your knee parallel to the floor.
5. Press the front hipbone forward and slightly extend the hip.
6. Repeat with the left leg.

ILIOTIBIAL BAND

1. Stand with your left hand on your left hip and your right arm over your head.
2. Cross your left foot over your right.
3. With your left hand, push your left hip to the right.
4. Repeat on the right side.

HIP FLEXORS

1. Kneel on your right leg with your left leg extended in front of you, foot flat on the floor.
2. Place your hands on your hips and contract your abdominals while keeping your back straight and your chest up.
3. Slowly transfer your weight to your left foot while simultaneously contracting the right gluteal area.
4. Lean toward the left.
5. Repeat on the other side.

HAMSTRINGS—OFF THE BIKE

1. Place your right foot on a step (or on the floor in front of you) with the knee slightly bent.
2. Lean forward from the hinge of the hip.
3. Your left knee will be slightly bent (the left leg is supporting your weight).

4. Press your buttocks and back up, pushing the hips away from the front knee.
5. Hold for 30 seconds to the point of a moderate stretch.
6. Repeat with the other leg.

HAMSTRINGS—ON THE BIKE

1. While riding, stand on the pedals so your feet are horizontal to the ground.
2. Flex the knees about 20 degrees and lean forward from the waist bringing your chest over the headset on the bike.
3. Hold for 30 seconds and then rotate the pedal 180 degrees.
4. Repeat.

GASTROCNEMIUS-SOLEUS—OFF THE BIKE

1. Stand facing a wall.
2. Squat down and place the heel of your right foot as near the wall as possible.
3. Stand up with your palms on the wall.
4. Move your chest toward the wall.
5. Hold for 30 seconds.
6. Repeat with your left heel close to the wall.

GASTROCNEMIUS-SOLEUS—ON THE BIKE

1. While coasting on your bike at any time or before the transition to the run, move slightly forward on the saddle.
2. Straighten one leg and lower the heel below the ball of the foot.
3. Hold for 5 to 10 seconds.
4. Repeat on the other side.

LOWER BACK—OFF THE BIKE

1. Kneel and place your palms on the floor directly in front of you.
2. Lean down toward the floor, tucking your head between your knees.
3. Arch your lower back.
4. Hold for 30 seconds.

LOWER BACK—ON THE BIKE

1. While coasting slowly, stand on the pedals with your hands stabilized on the bars.
2. Tuck your chin down and arch your back.
3. Hold for 30 seconds.

NECK

1. Move your head forward, lightly pushing your chin down toward your chest. Hold for 5 seconds on the bike or 30 seconds on the ground.
2. Lean your head back. Again, hold for 5 seconds on the bike or 30 seconds on the ground.
3. While shrugging your shoulders, lean to the left and then the right, holding for 5 or 30 seconds on each side.

Race-Ready Cycling Preparation

Triathletes need to develop a strategy for each leg of a triathlon. In the cycling leg, the event's distance, topography, environment, and competition are areas in which tactics certainly come into play. The intensity you choose to use for the bike portion will depend on your cycling-specific fitness and training preparation. If you go out too hard, your fat metabolism will take over quickly and you won't have enough energy left for the run that follows the cycling portion. If you go out too easy, you increase the length of time you need to complete the course, which also uses up additional carbohydrate stores.

Drafting Versus Time Trialing

If you're a professional triathlete, road-race drafting training is, of course, an essential part of the mix. Triathlon draft-legal racing is much different from cycling road racing in that there isn't much (if any) team strategy and the pace is more constant. You require significantly less energy to ride in the draft of one or a group of triathletes, however, and this is where strategy is very important.

I do not know of any draft-legal competitions for amateurs, although many triathletes blatantly ignore the rules. Non-drafting triathlons are to be competed in as individuals, without the advantages of drafting another cyclist. It is therefore important if you work out with a group to train frequently up front so you aren't drafting another cyclist. Significant postural differences in nondrafting riding methods must be developed by amateur triathletes, particularly the aero-bar position on the bike. While drafting, the energy output is not only lessened, but the body position of the rider is more upright, keeping a keen eye on the flow of the pace line and looking out for changes in pace in order to maintain balance and tempo within the pack. During a time trial, in contrast, the triathlete will be in the aero-bar position for much of if not the entire course. On courses that require you to hold your body in the aero position for extended periods, it becomes very important for you to have trained for that position so your body can make the right adaptations.

Transition Training

I like triathletes to train for their transitions in preparation for competition. In the early, base preparation phases, these transition-training sessions tend to be aerobic in nature to facilitate general fitness adaptation as well as sport-specific training of the swim-to-bike and bike-to-run transitions. As race preparation season arrives, the intensity and specificity of transition-training workouts increase.

Gearing

Choosing the right chainring and cassette for a course is an important part of the quick decision-making process that you'll want to hone during training so it will become automatic in a race situation. Normally, your overall fitness will determine whether you should consider making any modifications based on the profile of the bike course; knowing the right shifting sequence will keep your "engine" running smoothly by managing your energy output more efficiently. So be sure to practice calculating gearing ratios before the event.

Of course, if the cycling leg is hilly, flat, or at altitude or if it involves long climbs, descents, high or low temperatures, or something similar, tactical preparation becomes a key consideration. Conditions can vary widely throughout a single event. Being race-ready means that you have trained for conditions similar to those you will race in. If you can, ride the course before race day. This planning and practice will not only ready you, it will also provide useful tactical information such as gearing choices and the opportunity to assess your strengths and weaknesses.

Climbing, Descending, and Cornering Skills

With the wide array of aero bars on the market, proper hand positioning while climbing isn't so absolute. There are a number of choices depending on the manufacturer. However, you should choose a setup that complements your strengths while climbing. For many people, the seated position works best, so a bar configuration that allows for a center handhold is important. If you're like me and stand frequently on long climbs in a low gear spinning at a high cadence, you may find the brake-hood position more comfortable.

Still others like a combination of standing and sitting, so your hand-position preferences are something to determine and practice in training so you can be comfortable when racing.

Be aware that in the aero-bar position, you may not have an unfettered reach to the brakes. This can be dangerous when you're descending steep, sharp switchbacks or cornering. It is important to be as stable as possible on your bike and to have the ability to abruptly dampen your speed by "feathering" the brakes (figure 3.5).

On steep descents with sharp turns, place your hands so they can easily reach and feather-touch the brakes as they also provide steady support to the body. Also, come into turns on the apex with the inside crank at the top and the inside knee leaning outward. The other crank will be down at the bottom of the stroke, supporting about 70 percent of your weight. You won't need to turn the aero bars at high speeds because shifting your weight and leaning will turn the bike.

© Craig Melvin/SportsChrome

Figure 3.5   Excellent cornering posture.

CHAPTER 4

Effortless Running

Ultimately, much of the improvement a triathlete can make in her performance comes from developing and maintaining strength, flexibility, and neuromuscular coordination. Stretching, specific strength work, and running drills therefore are essential for the triathlete's training routine.

Improving one's running isn't as simple as it may seem. You'll have to practice to learn how to run efficiently, with special emphasis on strengthening your core muscles and focusing on your technique (especially posture). Running efficiently is especially important for triathletes because after they complete the swimming and cycling segments, fatigue and diminishing energy stores heighten the demands of running.

It's easy to spot a triathlete runner with good form in a pack of runners with less efficient form. Good runners make it look almost effortless with their smooth, relaxed strides and upper-body movements; their stable, balanced posture; and little up-and-down or side-to-side movement. Learning to run faster and more efficiently begins with understanding basic mechanical concepts and applying those to your unique style of running.

To improve efficiency, you have to reduce the amount of energy you expend to run. Impressive improvement in performance time is associated with energy-expenditure decrease. So just how do you improve the economy of your running movement? You have to train to increase your functional coordination (improve neuromuscular movement), strengthen your core (abdominals and back), lessen or eliminate wasteful movements, and decrease vertical while increasing horizontal velocity.

Improving Running Biomechanics

Although an athletic posture is a central theme in each event of a triathlon, it is perhaps never more important than with running. During a triathlon, efficiency of movement is central to achieving your best performance times. The buildup of fatigue from swimming and cycling heighten the physical (and emotional) demands placed on the runner biomechanically. It is here that effective technique and running posture will become your best friends.

Achieving an athletic running posture requires sufficient functional strength and neuromuscular coordination. The functional strength themes that were described in detail in chapter 1 lead the way to improved performance in swimming, cycling, and running. In this chapter, we will address techniques for the development of neuromuscular coordination and provide drills and specific tips to help you run better.

Of the few biomechanical differences between walking and running, the primary one is that when we run, we are airborne for a short time. Because of this, it is important that your upper body be stabilized over your pelvis and leaning forward only a little. Leaning too far forward restrains stride mechanics by increasing the vertical forces at foot strike, so it is vital to maintain balance and postural support with every stride over any type of topography.

Improving body alignment while running requires keeping your center of body mass over the support leg at foot strike. You can achieve this ideal alignment by incorporating the following into your running mechanics:

- Keep your hips forward by slightly tightening your gluteal muscles.
- Position your earlobes over your shoulders.
- Hold your chin up so it is parallel with the ground at all times.
- Hold your chest high by gently contracting your shoulder blades and keeping your back straight.
- Keep your center of mass over your support leg at each foot strike.
- Relaxation of the upper body is an essential aspect of efficient running. Lessen any muscular tension in the upper torso (especially on hills) and economy will improve. Keep the upper body soft, supple, and settled over the pelvis with the back straight, chin level with the ground, and the chest up.

Each runner has complexly interrelated, unique biomechanical characteristics, which means that not all techniques work for everyone. The differences among runners include their level of experience as well as their muscle lengths, strength, gait alignment, injuries, and other functional limitations. Once again, a functional assessment by a physical therapist can be of significant value in customizing drills and techniques and identifying the muscle-length issues to focus on.

Drills are a cornerstone of learning to run more efficiently. Perfecting your running mechanics with these drills ultimately will reduce the amount of energy you'll have to expend to run a given speed—and that's a good thing. Later in this chapter, we'll review running drills I developed for or found to be beneficial in teaching triathletes how to engage their muscles to fire at the right times.

Head and Shoulder Position

While running, align your head with your spine and your ears with your shoulders: Where the head goes, the spine follows (figure 4.1). Lowering your head will unbalance your body weight and require more energy expenditure as you attempt to stabilize yourself with each foot strike. Try to keep your head in a neutral position over your spine and your eyes looking ahead of you at a point just below the horizon. The goal is to allow the head and neck to rest atop the upper trunk and shoulders, staying relaxed.

© Harry How/Getty Images

Figure 4.1   Ironman champion Peter Reid displays outstanding posture.

Athletic relaxation comes with practice, but perhaps even more so with core and functional strength. As you gain functional running experience, flexibility, and strength, the economy of your movements will improve. Here are a few tips for increasing relaxation while you're running:

1. Keep your facial muscles, particularly your jawbone, loose and relaxed.

2. Don't grind your teeth.

3. Relax your fingers, hands, wrists, and arms so they effortlessly coordinate with your leg movements.

4. Don't focus your eyes on any object or person.

5. Keep your shoulders relaxed and low—don't let them rise up.

Arm Carriage

The arms are not just for balance, they also contribute—albeit only a small amount—to your running speed by helping to maintain constant coordinated motion to propel you forward. Try running with your arms held at your sides to see how important your arms are for efficient running.

Your arms help to propel you forward by moving back and forth at your sides. Keep your arms very relaxed and bent at about 90 to 100 degrees. Loosely cup your hands and relax your wrists. Pull your elbow straight back (or slightly to the outside) until your little finger is even with your hip. During forward arm recovery, bring your hand to near the middle of your chest, but do not cross it. All the while, keep your muscles relaxed and maintain smooth, quick, light foot strikes.

If you're running at your best, it is likely that your movements are forward, not lateral. If your arms cross the midline of your chest, they increase the lateral forces that your body must counterbalance to direct that energy forward. That, of course, increases the energy costs of running without benefiting performance.

Many years ago, I learned a constructive running technique from Jim Hunt, a noted track coach in Northern California. He likened the hand and wrist movements in running to holding and pounding drumsticks. This analogy makes a lot of sense to me, as it does to many of the athletes I have trained to make their arm carriage more efficient. Because the arms work in coordination with the legs, using this drumbeat analogy can also help control the stride rate tempo. Move your arms quickly and your legs will follow. Instead of counting foot strikes, as noted in the following section, you can count "drumbeats." If you count 180 or more beats per minute, you're on track for an optimal cadence.

Foot Strike

I don't endorse the practice of heel striking, as some coaches, magazine articles, and triathletes and runners do. Heel striking results in a braking force during the running stride that sends forces vertically rather than horizontally, which is the direction you want to go. Many recreational runners demonstrate what I mean by a braking force. Novice runners often have low stride frequencies (stride rate) and long stride lengths, making it likely that the lower leg and foot extend beyond the center of mass at foot strike (generally, beyond the knee). This slows down their forward momentum because each time the heel strikes the ground, the resultant forces are directed upward.

Instead, I recommend that athletes strive for either a full-footed (flat-footed), midsole, or forefoot foot strike directly underneath their center of mass. Making a deliberate effort to land full-footed at foot strike generates the greatest amount of forward thrust (horizontal velocity) and lessens the braking forces that increase energy expenditure and slow you down. Land under the center of your body's mass to minimize deceleration and increase forward propulsion. To build up your foot muscles and neuromuscular agility, be sure to do the excellent plyometric foot drills described in chapter 1.

Forward-Swing Phase

The period from the toe-off to when the leg swings forward is one in which I feel triathletes can gain substantial forward drive. This phase is in reality a period of recovery, because the push-off momentum accelerates the leg forward. I coach my athletes to reduce the airborne time by increasing the speed of the forward swing. The result is a rapid toe-off-to-foot-contact time and therefore an increased stride rate. There is little or no additional oxygen use.

To accomplish this, concentrate on bringing your heel forward and under your buttocks as quickly as possible. A good way to learn it is to walk rapidly not by pushing off harder or taking longer steps, but by toeing off and accelerating the recovery by getting the foot back on the ground as quickly as possible.

Stride Length

Studies indicate that runners optimize their own stride length when they run. Triathletes, however, may not achieve their optimal stride length if they have restrictions in flexibility or strength. The hip flexor, gastrocnemius, and gluteal muscles and the hamstrings need to have their full ranges of motion to maximize stride length.

If the hip flexors are tight, both knee lift and forward flexion following the push-off of the stride are restricted, which in turn lessen the extension of the opposite leg during the stance to toe-off phases. At toe-off, your pelvis and femur (thigh) should be aligned (figure 4.2). Ideally, if you're a triathlete or a distance runner, you should not lift your knee too high, but rather bring it forward and upward to about 45 degrees and give more forward and horizontal movement to your thigh following toe-off.

On the whole, what you need to do is improve flexibility and strength to maximize stride length without compromising stride frequency. To do this properly, try to improve your thrust and momentum. As a result, you'll cover a greater distance, but your stride rate will remain the same.

Figure 4.2   Pelvis-femur alignment at toe-off.

Stride Frequency

In elite distance runners, foot-strike contact time with the ground is very brief—just a few milliseconds. As we've already discussed, you should strive for a foot strike on the midsole or the forefoot (not the heel) to direct the resulting forces horizontally for quick and very efficient "push back" or "pawing." The accepted stride rate for fast distance running is more than 180 strides per minute (90 to 92 for each leg). Generally, I look for triathletes to achieve a rate close to this on all types of terrain.

Consequently, when stride frequency is too high or low or stride lengths are too short or long, the horizontal force generated (i.e., your running speed) is reduced. Each foot contact with the ground should be forcefully applied but smoothly distributed as the foot "claws" the ground, propelling your body forward. Midfoot contact is the best way to achieve this, as opposed to a heel strike, which substantially increases ground forces (braking forces), reduces forward propulsion, and increases vertical forces.

Running Drills

With all running drills, the goal is functional stability and coordination. Running drills help reinforce posture and proprioceptive awareness and increase neuromuscular development of joint, limb, and muscular movements. Maintain a tall trunk posture with your chest up, back straight, ears over your shoulders, chin parallel with the ground, and transverse abdominals contracted during each of the drills.

Drill training can be done as part of a limbering-up session before, during, or after training sessions or before competitions. In addition, setting aside a specific, weekly drill-training workout as I've done in the program that follows is an excellent addition to any triathlete's program.

The running segment of triathlon is time and again the linchpin of the event. Without a solid run, there is not much hope of reaching a best time outcome or the podium. Again and again, it is the fundamentals of technique, core strength, and the athlete's consistent application and development of those skills that truly make the difference. To that end, drills work on running mechanics by isolating the muscles of the hip, back, calves, arms, shoulders, hamstrings, quadriceps, feet, and ankles that are used in running fast.

SEATED ARM SWING

Works functional arm positioning at varying swing speeds. Also excellent for training posture.

1. Sit up straight with your back against a pole for support and your chest up. Extend your legs straight in front, keeping your toes pointed at the ceiling.

2. Flex your arms 90 degrees at your sides (as you do when running). You may hold a 2- or 5-pound dumbbell in each hand.

3. Slowly begin swinging your arms forward and backward in the same movement that you use when running. Pull your elbows straight back or just slightly to the outside and let your arms swing forward to the middle of your chest. Be sure your shoulders are relaxed.

4. Gradually increase the speed in stages (i.e., 80 percent, then 85, then 90 percent, and so on) and hold each stage for 15 seconds; then incrementally reduce your speed, again pausing at each stage for 15 seconds.

5. It's OK to allow your feet and legs to move sideways a bit, but keep your legs straight (although relaxed) and your toes pointing toward the ceiling.

DYNAMIC ANKLE DEVELOPMENT

Develops ankle strength, flexibility, and proprioceptive coordination. Walk for 10 m while performing each of the drills.

1. Walk on your heels, pulling your toes toward your shins.
2. Walk on the balls of your feet (making yourself as tall as possible).
3. Walk on the outer sides of your feet.
4. Walk on the inner sides of your feet.

HIP EXTENSION AND FLEXION

Improves hip extension and flexion, which are important for reaching the full range of motion during the push off and forward swing in running.

1. Stand with your arms outstretched and your hands placed flat against a wall.

2. Move your left foot forward (closer to the wall) and balance it on a disk pillow with your knee flexed slightly. Completely extend your right leg behind you (away from the wall).

3. Gradually move your right thigh forward and upward a few inches, making the movement from the hip.

4. Then accelerate the forward movement, quickly bringing your thigh up and your hip to full flexion.

5. Now, extend your right leg as far back as possible, touching the floor with your toe.

6. Do 10, 20, or 30 repetitions and then switch legs.

7. Once you have mastered this drill at a wall, try it with your hands on a chair. Another option is to face away from a wall, with one end of a length of tubing attached to your ankle and the other end attached to the wall at hip height. Doing so increases resistance and improves proprioceptive coordination.

MARCH TO CLAW

Enhances proprioceptive stabilization along with neuromuscular control when performing the support-to-toe-off phase.

1. Stand with your left leg on a disk pillow and raise your right thigh until it is parallel with the floor (the march position).
2. Stabilize your body by contracting and holding in the transverse abdominals for five seconds.
3. Flex your left knee two or three inches.
4. Rapidly lower your right foot, clawing at the floor by brushing over it with the ball of your foot.
5. Quickly return to the march position for 10 repetitions, then switch sides.

PRANCING QUICK FEET TO FULL FOOT

Works on foot proprioception, strength, agility, and coordination. Generally used as part of a warm-up.

1. Begin by quickly and lightly running in place (quick feet) on the balls of your feet.
2. Move your arms in synchronization with your feet.
3. Progressively move forward in short, quick steps from the ball of the foot to the mid-sole, and eventually stomp the ground with your full foot for six to ten repetitions.
4. Vary the intensity of the stomping over the 15, 20, or 30 seconds that you'll perform this drill.

SINGLE-LEGGED HOP

Develops proprioceptive balance and strength in the hip, quadriceps, foot, and shin.

1. Place your right thigh in the march position (parallel with the floor).
2. Lower and touch your right toes and ball of the foot to the ground, then rapidly swing your right thigh upward toward chest height. The left foot will come off the floor when done correctly.
3. Repeat 5 to 10 times with each leg.

HIGH-KNEE SKIPPING

An excellent drill for developing knee, hip, foot, and arm coordination.

1. Skip in place, alternating the right and left legs, with the trailing leg hopping on each skip.
2. Gradually begin running forward while skipping; increase the height of the thigh lift with each stride.
3. Move your arms at the same rate as your legs as you maintain a tall pose: your back straight, your chin up, and your shoulders relaxed.
4. Skip, exaggerating the height of each skip, for 25 m. Then skip for 25 m more, exaggerating the length of each skip by skipping as far as possible. Skip with the right leg, then skip with the left leg.

HEEL KICK-UP

Good for foot dynamics training, arm coordination, and posture.

1. Begin jogging lightly, bringing your heel(s) up to your buttocks. NOTE: Single- or double-heel kick-ups can be performed.

2. Rapidly get off the foot, working the arms in coordination with each heel lift.

3. Try including single-legged kick-ups, performed by rapidly bringing the right heel repeatedly to the butt. On the jog back, do the same, but with the left heel.

MARCH WALKING AND RUNNING KICK-OUT

Contributes to balance and coordination of the lower and upper body. Also good for kinesthetic development of hip extension when done single-legged. Generally used as part of a warm-up.

1. Begin walking slowly, raising your knees higher with each step.

2. Once your thigh is at hip level, hold for five seconds and then kick out the lower leg, keeping your foot flexed and your toes toward your shin.

3. Perform as described while walking or running, single- and double-legged.

HIGH-KNEE FORM ACCELERATION

An excellent series for improving form mechanics, neuromuscular development, and body balance. Provides an opportunity to run for short time periods at very fast speeds. Has outstanding benefits for technique, stride rate, arm carriage, body posture, and stride length.

1. Begin running and gradually increase the tempo.
2. Raise the knees and thighs to a higher level (no more than above chest height) every 10 seconds.
3. Your hand should reach your chest and return to your hip during each gait cycle.
4. Maintain posture throughout the acceleration interval (generally, 10 to 40 seconds).
5. Follow with light, relaxed running.

SIDEWAYS RUNNING

Limbers the body and develops nonlinear muscle groups, proprioceptive coordination, and stability. Generally used as part of a warm-up.

1. Begin with your hands at your sides.
2. As you take a sideways step, simultaneously raise your arms and hands to above shoulder height.
3. Continue taking steps sideways until you are running sideways; squat down with each step as you raise your arms and hands overhead. Another way of visualizing this drill is to think of making "angels" in the snow, except, of course, you're standing and moving.

SINGLE-LEGGED PLYO-JUMP

Develops hip flexor, gluteal, and quadriceps strength and proprioceptive stability.

1. At the bottom of a grassy slope of 5 to 10 or more degrees, step forward onto the slope with your left foot with your right leg slightly flexed and behind you.
2. Squat down onto the left leg about two to four inches.
3. Now, thrust upward on your left foot, landing about six inches higher up the slope.
4. Continue up the slope for three to five repetitions with the left leg, then switch to the right leg.

ALTERNATE LEG BOUND

An exceptional dry land and running drill for proprioception as well as hip flexor, gluteal, quadriceps, and foot strength.

1. Begin with your left leg in front of your right.
2. Push off the right leg, energetically bringing the thigh and knee forward and upward.
3. Return to the starting position, then switch leg positions and repeat the sequence.

ALTERNATE LEG BOX STEP

Great for foot, hip, and gastrocnemius-soleus coordination and strength development.

1. Stand facing a 12- to 18-inch-high step box that is against a wall. The box should be able to support at least half of your weight.
2. Place your right foot and about 20 percent of your weight on the box.
3. Now, quickly switch feet and continue alternating them for 30 seconds.

Warm-Up Transition Drills

Drills can be done at any time during most runs. They need not be "saved" for the track. Many athletes I coach use drills as a dynamic warm-up before supplemental training. In the drills we just learned, I pointed out the ones that often are used for warming up, and here's a typical sequence that not only warms the muscles effectively, but helps you work on your running form as well.

Jog for one minute.

Perform three sets of 15 seconds of each of the following:

- Prancing Quick Feet to Full Foot
- High-Knee Skipping
- Sideways Running
- Backward Running
- High-Knee Form Accelerations
- Pelvic Roll-Ups (abdominals, 15 repetitions) as described in chapter 5
- Push-Ups (10 to 20 repetitions)

Jog for one minute.

Perform the following stretches for 30 seconds each:

- Hip Flexors
- Calves
- Hamstrings
- Quadriceps

Jog for one minute.

Perform three sets of 20 seconds of each of the following:

- Dynamic foot drills, such as the heel, toe, inner sides, and outer sides
- Heel Kick-Ups
- March Walking and Running Kick-Outs
- Seated Arm Swing
- Alternate Leg Bound
- VMO Squats (hold for 10 seconds on each of 15 repetitions—see chapter 5)

Do two sets of the following stretches, performing each for 30 seconds:

- Hip Flexors
- Calves
- Hamstrings
- Quadriceps

High-Knee Form Accelerations

Do four repetitions of a 20-second acceleration plus a 40-second jog.

Race-Ready Running

As the final event of the triathlon, the race-running strategy is distinctive from that used in the swimming and cycling segments. In the early 1980s, several triathlons were organized with the run first, followed by the bike race and finishing with the swim. Participants in these contests found the sequence to be an eye-opener, to say the least. When they hit the water following the running and cycling time trials, the first thing they noticed was that their blood had pooled in their legs, making their arms feel like feathers and their legs feel like lead. For many, this resulted in a slanted, legs-downward position when they first entered the water, making swimming nearly impossible for a time. Needless to say, this format did not prove to be popular, because wetsuits, which could have provided some buoyancy, were not used at that time, and weaker swimmers were nearly drowning, or at least could manage to swim only for survival, rather than to race.

The triathlon's set swim-bike-run format today means that during the running segment, triathletes experience similar changes in biomechanics as a result of residual fatigue from the swimming and biking portions. Recognizing the effects of this fatigue on your running form can help you run your best during the race. In my opinion, the two most important factors to recognize and train for in preparing the athlete for race fatigue are running posture and stride rate.

Professional world-class triathletes are now running the Olympic triathlon running distance of 10K in under 5 minutes per mile for the men and 5:30 for the women. This demonstrates the substantial progress triathletes are making as the sport matures. It will be interesting when the Ironman Hawaii marathon times for the men reach this same high mark. After all these years, Mark Allen's and Dave Scott's 1989 Ironman Hawaii marathon records still stand.

Racing Posture Focus

The stance of the body while running is very important during a triathlon because fatigue definitely becomes a factor during the run. Maintaining a tall, athletic body position is fundamental to running at your best. To do this, make sure your back is straight, your chin is up, and your chest is high. Also, keep your ears over your shoulders—don't deviate from this regardless of the terrain or how you feel. This position promotes the most efficient use of energy. During a race, bring your hands over your head and behind your neck from time to time. This straightens the back and raises the chest and chin. Hold this position for only a few strides, then bring the arms back to the sides, maintaining the high posture. Using this technique during longer runs and doing the drills described previously in this chapter as well as the abdominal exercises described in chapter 5 will help ensure that race fatigue does not affect your running posture.

Stride Rate and Length Focus

During the bike phase of a triathlon, your rpm will likely be somewhere between 90 and 100. The best running stride rate is about 90 to 93 strides per minute, so there really isn't much difference here. Of course, each event involves different muscle groups, which is why the bike-to-run transition workouts are important throughout the season, and even more important as key competitions draw near.

Keep in mind that after coming right off the bike, you will tend to over-stride in the first few running strides. This takes too much energy and dispro-portionately emphasizes the thigh muscles. Focus on starting with a shorter, faster stride instead, which works most effectively by using the hip flexors, hamstrings, gluteals, and gastrocnemius-soleus of the lower legs. Coming off the bike, your legs will find these shorter strides a much-appreciated change of muscle-group usage.

Race Course Awareness

Familiarity with the running course is essential in race-day preparation. You need to know the landmarks of the course not only so you won't take a wrong turn and can plan your pace and strategy, but also so you can pre-pare your body for the terrain. Before a race, be sure your training program includes runs over similar terrain, whether the course includes steep uphills or downhills or rolling or flat terrain.

Group Training

Occasionally training with a group of runners is a good idea for learning how to manage your own intensity levels and also to push yourself. During the early part of the season (base preparation, see chapter 7), plan to run with a group on an overdistance run every three weeks. Doing a group run more fre-quently may result in the run becoming either too competitive or too com-fortable; many athletes will "settle" into a pace with an intensity that is either too high or too low and may not be beneficial to your base development. In the race preparation phase, working with a group more often (at least once weekly) is a great idea. Again, however, change the venue from the track to the trail so there's variability in training. Group trail running can be a lot of fun and is more race-specific than running on a track each week.

Nutrition Strategies

Nutrition strategies are a bit different on the run than in the other two phases of the triathlon and of course depend on the length of competition time. Heart and respiration rates tend to be a bit higher on the run than on the bike, making it less comfortable to consume solid foods. Fortunately, there are many different energy gels on the market to choose from. Most of them contain similar amounts of carbohydrates, of which you should try to take in about 40 to 60 grams per hour from all sources—energy drinks, gels, and bars or other items. Any more will delay gastric absorption and increase fatigue.

In terms of fluid replacement, do not have a stomach full of fluids during the run. For this reason alone, it's very important to stay on a regular fluid-intake timetable. Take in 4 to 8 ounces (a couple of mouthfuls) every 10 to 15 minutes. Drink small quantities regularly to maintain a more consistent performance. A mere 1 percent loss in total body water results in a lower maximal oxygen capacity. A 3 percent loss significantly impairs performance, and a 4 percent loss increases effort, discomfort, and pulse and respiratory rates and slows the pace.

CHAPTER 5

Functional Strength and Triathlon Performance

Perhaps the most important addition to my supplemental program over the past few years has been the inclusion of functional stabilization exercises to strengthen and balance the triathlete's foundation. Any athlete with a weak core or muscle group compensates for that weakness by using less efficient movements. Triathletes who've developed their functional strength throughout their core muscles and who've developed their proprioceptive balance—the body's way of maintaining stability and orientation during static and dynamic activities—are at a decided advantage over those who haven't.

The core's chief function is to maintain postural control by stabilizing the body's center of gravity during running, swimming, cycling, and weight training. The more functional strength you have, the better your efficiency. So, whatever your athletic level, supplemental dryland training that focuses on functional stabilization is perhaps the most important training you can do. The dryland program and exercises outlined in this chapter are specifically for triathletes and have evolved over my 20 years of coaching triathletes. Many, if not all, of the exercises can be performed using a stability ball (Swiss ball) and stabilization (disk) pads, which add the element of balance to the exercises—that is, the body not only has to lift the weight, it also has to balance itself while doing so. This balancing while strengthening better simulates the work the muscles have to do when you are swimming, cycling, and running.

Muscle strength plays an important role in performance and the ability to put up with the demands that multisport training places upon the body. Muscle strength developed beyond the functional needs of the triathlete, however, may be of less benefit and, in the case of overly increased muscle mass, even inhibit triathlon performance.

The kind of muscular strength training we're about to discuss is not the same as that used by weight lifters, football players, wrestlers, high jumpers, or 100 m sprinters. Rather, the type of strength training triathletes need is specifically aimed at the development, enhancement, and maintenance of specialized strength for swimming, cycling, and running. For triathletes, strength need only be developed to a level that preserves endurance performance at peak levels. Increases in strength beyond that can be detrimental to performance.

Greater adaptations to sport performance require exercise to be highly specific. That is, to improve swimming, cycling, and running, a triathlete must practice those sports. The adaptations occur in both the cardiovascular and muscular (active) systems. In the musculoskeletal system, bone, muscle, and connective tissue increase their metabolic and force-generating capacities.

The most efficient movements are made when the body assumes an athletic, stable posture. This posture can be developed by boosting the flexibility, balance, and strength of the active (agonist) and supporting (antagonist) muscles in addition to learning skills and technique while maintaining this position. Swimming, cycling, and running skills benefit by preparing the supporting muscles of the core and trunk to stabilize movements and improve the efficiency of the movements.

Develop the specific type and amount of strength that will allow you to compete at your peak level.

Abdominal Core Exercises

I have designed the following core exercise program specifically for triathletes. The core is the single most important area of supplemental conditioning; exercises for the core—and in particular, those that involve using a stability ball—reduce muscular imbalance and increase proprioception and neuromuscular coordination in the abdominal and back muscles. Chapters 6 through 9 set out how to perform the exercises and detail the number of repetitions to do, the rest intervals, and the dryland phase in which each of the exercises is most appropriate. The dryland phases are divided into different periods, each having a particular training emphasis.

Be sure to draw in your lower abdominal muscles during all of the following exercises. The correct size of stability ball for you should put your thighs slightly higher than your hips when you sit on it. Of course, many different-sized balls can be used once stability and movement control improve.

V-UP AND OVER

1. Lie on your back and grip a medicine ball between your ankles.
2. Use your abdominal muscles to raise your legs and arms simultaneously so they meet together in the middle to form a V.
3. Now anchor your arms on the floor out to each side while keeping your legs up.
4. Slowly move the leg to the right and left, up to about 18 inches.
5. Return the legs to the floor and repeat.

QUADRIPLEX CONTRALATERAL EXTENSION

1. Start by positioning yourself on your hands and knees with your head hanging. Wearing ankle and wrist weights is optional.
2. Draw in the transversus abdominis (lower abdominal muscle). This feels like "sucking in" the lower part of your belly.
3. Raise your head and neck, left arm, and right leg to full extension (parallel with the floor) and lift your chin.
4. Hold for 30 seconds.
5. Lower your head and neck, arm, and leg.
6. Repeat on the other side.

BACK EXTENSION

1. Lie face down with your hips on a stability or Swiss ball.
2. Place both of your feet against a wall with your feet spread wider than the width of your shoulders.
3. Raise and lower your torso from the hips and cross your hands over your chest. This is called a "center extension."
4. Next, vary the movement by raising yourself to a single side or alternating from side to side. You can make this exercise more challenging by holding a medicine ball.

STABILITY BALL CRUNCH

1. Sit on a stability ball and roll or walk your body down it until the ball hits the arch of your back.

2. Keep your feet on the ground at a little more than hip-width apart and your eyes looking at a spot on the ceiling at all times.

3. Cross your arms across your chest or hold a barbell with a wide snatch grip. Other options are holding a medicine ball over your head with both hands (pictured), or one hand, on your shoulders, or on your chest.

4. Contract the obliques (internal and external) while raising your chest toward the ceiling. Focus on a spot on the ceiling. The crunch is complete when your obliques have fully contracted (at the end of the range of contraction, the muscular intensity decreases).

5. Crunch to the center for 4 to 10 repetitions, then crunch to the right shoulder and then the left shoulder for 4 to 10 repetitions each.

6. As your skill level improves, lift one leg off the floor for half of the repetitions and then the other leg for the other half.

PELVIC ROLL-UP

1. Lie on your back with your feet on the floor and your knees up. You may also perform this exercise with a disk pillow under the arch of your back. (See www.performbetter.com for information on where to buy a disk pillow.)

2. Preset the abdominal muscles by drawing in the transversus abdominis. Focus on a spot on the ceiling to keep your chin up.

3. Place a medicine ball between your knees.

4. Raise both knees by using your abdominal muscles and rotating your pelvis.

5. When the transversus abdominis is fully contracted, pause and lift both of your knees one inch higher toward the ceiling.

HANGING LEG RAISE WITH MEDICINE BALL

1. Use elbow straps to hang from a chin-up bar.

2. Draw in the transversus abdominis.

3. Raise both knees to your chest, then to your right and left sides, and then to the pike position, keeping your feet swinging and your legs even with your hips. To increase the difficulty, place a medicine ball between your ankles.

4. Hold each position for several seconds.

ISOLATERAL FLEXION AND EXTENSION

1. Lie on your left side on the floor or with your feet on a disk pillow or a stability ball, bridging up onto your left forearm.

2. Contract the transversus abdominis.

3. Extend the non-bridging right arm at shoulder height.

4. Slowly bring the right knee toward the chest (flexion) and then extend the leg from the hip (extension).

5. Repeat on the other side.

6. You can also perform this exercise by holding a medicine ball at arm's length from your body at varying locations (pictured) or having your coach toss the ball to you.

PRONE BRIDGE

1. Lying prone (face down) on the floor, bridge up onto your forearms, raising your hips off the floor.
2. Draw in the transversus abdominis while keeping your hips and back straight.
3. You may also try this with your feet on a bench or stability ball.

SINGLE-ARMED BALL BRIDGE

1. Place your left hand at the top of a medicine or stability ball. Put your right hand on the side of the ball. Your feet should be on the floor about six inches apart.
2. Step back until your hips are level and contract the transversus abdominis muscle.
3. Slowly raise your right arm out to the side and hold it there for 5 to 10 seconds.
4. Try performing the same exercise while standing on one leg.

Note: Beginners should skip step 3 and instead simply hold the extended position, with both of your hands on the ball, for 5 to 10 seconds. Then roll the ball about two inches forward, return, roll two inches to the right, two to the left, and two backward, keeping your feet in the same place.

FIVE-WAY ROLLOUT SERIES

1. Lie face down with your forearms on a stability ball, your feet on the floor, and your back straight. Very slowly extend your forearms (a). Repeat 5 to 10 times.

2. Lie face down. Slowly "walk" over the ball with your hands until your shins and ankles lie on the stability ball. Complete a push-up (or several).

3. Pike at the hips, moving onto the tips of your toes on the stability ball, then lower your hips and raise first your left and then your right leg for five seconds each (b).

5. Finally, bring both knees forward to your chest several times, rolling the ball beneath your shins (c).

6. Once you have mastered this routine using both legs, try the sequence using only one leg.

a

b

c

SINGLE-LEGGED STEP BOX STABILITY BALL ROLLOUTS

1. Place your forearms on the stability ball with your back to a step box or bench.
2. Lift one leg behind you onto the step box, followed by the other leg.
3. Hold this position for 5 to 10 seconds, then extend (raise) one leg a few inches off the step box. Repeat with the other leg.
4. Now, with both feet on the step box and your forearms on the stability ball, roll two inches forward, to the right, to the left, and backward.

TRANSVERSUS ABDOMINIS

1. Lie on your back with your feet on the floor and your knees pointing up.
2. Place a deflated blood pressure cuff under your lower back.
3. Inflate the cuff to 40 to 50 mmHg.
4. Draw in the muscles of the lower abdomen without using the muscles of the back. If you can feel the cuff move, your back muscles are too active. Contract the lower abdominals more and more.
5. Next, raise your left knee six to eight inches toward your chest and hold that position for five seconds. Again, if the cuff moves, this indicates too much use of the back muscles and not enough of the transversus abdominis.
6. Repeat, raising your right leg to your chest and holding.

Weight and Stability Ball Training

The following exercises combine or modify traditional weight training exercises with others I have developed independently for the functional movements of triathletes.

Many of the weight exercises start and finish in similar positions, which is important for completing the movements optimally, safely, and functionally. A lot can be said for having a professional trainer observe your movements to help you adjust incorrect and possibly dangerous movements. To this end, also follow these key points to ensure that you achieve the proper athletic posture during Olympic platform, barbell, and dumbbell training.

1. Grip the bar just outside your hips.
2. Flex your knees slightly.
3. Straighten your back.
4. Keep your chest up and your shoulder blades squeezed medially.
5. Place your feet shoulder-width apart.
6. Distribute your weight slightly more toward your heels.
7. Start and finish each exercise in one functional movement. Do not hinge at the waist to pick up or place the weights on the floor.

Chest and Back

The chest and back muscles need frequent, regular, consistent strength training as a supplement to triathlon-specific training. The body is an immense connected chain and if any one component breaks down, other areas of the body compensate, which often leads to injury. The powerful muscles of the chest (the greater and smaller pectorals) play an important role in swimming—they help to articulate the arm throughout the swimming stroke. Strengthening the back helps to balance the strength of the chest and abdominals and results in better athletic posture for all movements.

STABILITY BALL INCLINED PUSH-UP

1. Place your hands shoulder-width apart on a stability ball with your arms fully extended.
2. Extend your legs behind you with your feet staying flat on the floor. Or, for a more advanced move, place your feet (toes) on a bench or step box.
3. Slowly bend your elbows to lower your chest to the ball and return to the starting position.
4. Maintain an athletic posture throughout the movement with your chin up, back straight, ears over your shoulders, and chest up.

THREE-WAY STABILITY
AND MEDICINE BALL PUSH-UPS

1. Place two small medicine or stability balls of the same size side by side about a body's length from a large stability ball.
2. Lying face down over the stability ball, use your hands to walk out slowly to the small balls. Your ankles should be on the large ball when you've rolled out far enough.
3. Place your right hand on one of the small balls, then your left hand on the other, and press up.
4. Now do 5 to 15 push-ups.

Beginners can place their hands on the medicine balls and then roll back off the stability ball and repeat. Advanced athletes can perform the push-ups with one leg extended. The superadvanced can put three to five medicine balls side by side a body's length away and then walk their hands over to each ball, performing a push-up at every new position.

STABILITY BALL "BENCH" PRESS

1. Hold a barbell on your lap as you sit on a stability ball.
2. Walk forward with your feet until the ball is between your shoulder blades. Keep both feet on the floor and your knees bent.
3. Perform a bench press by raising the bar straight above your chest and then slowly lowering it to your chest.

DISK AND TUBING LATERAL FLY

1. Connect a 6- to 10-foot piece of elastic tubing (or exercise band) around a pole or thread it through an eye hook or carabiner at shoulder height. Hold each end of the band.

2. Step onto a disk pillow with your left foot by lunging forward onto it.

3. Begin from the "athletic posture" position and march, holding the tubing, as you extend both of your arms laterally.

4. Draw in the transverse abdominis throughout the movement.

STABILITY BALL FLEXED-ARM PULLOVER

1. Take a barbell (or two dumbbells) and sit on a stability ball, holding the weight in your hands on your lap.
2. Walk your feet forward on the ball until it is between your shoulder blades and your feet are flat on the floor.
3. Hold the barbell or dumbbells extended even with the shoulders and floor.
4. Arc the bar or dumbbells backward over your head and toward the floor, keeping your elbows flexed slightly (not locked out).
5. Stop when the weight is nearly even with your head.
6. Pull the weight back above your chest with your elbows flexed.

INCLINE STABILITY BALL DUMBBELL FLY OR PRESS-UP

1. Take two dumbbells and sit on a stability ball or inclined bench, holding the weight on your lap.
2. Lie back on the ball or bench and lift the weights over your head with your palms inward.
3. To do a fly, gently lower the weight to each side with your elbows slightly flexed until your elbows are even with your shoulders.
3. To do a press-up, begin in the same starting position and lower the weight straight down to your shoulders and then press up like you do in a bench press, but with your palms facing inward.

FRONT LATERAL PULL-DOWN

1. While standing, grab a cable bar in a wide overhand grip. (Use elastic tubing connected overhead as you sit on a stability ball if a lat machine is not available.)
2. Sit down on the seat with your feet flat on the floor and your arms overhead.
3. With your back straight and your shoulder blades slightly squeezed together, lean back about six inches.
4. Pull your elbows down and back using the muscles of the back.
5. Keep your elbows slightly flexed to keep them above your hands, simulating the downstroke of freestyle swimming.
6. Bring the bar down to your upper chest, then slowly return it to the overhead position and repeat.

CABLE LATERAL EXTENSION

1. While standing, grab a cable bar with a shoulder-width overhand grip.
2. Remain standing (or sit on a stability ball) and pull the weight, keeping your elbows above your hands, down to your hips.
3. Slowly return the bar to the starting position and repeat.

SEATED PULLEY ROW

1. Grab a pulley with your arms straight and sit on the floor with your legs extended, but your knees slightly bent.
2. Be sure your back is straight and your chest is up (squeeze your shoulder blades together).
3. Bend at the elbows and use your back muscles to pull the weight straight back toward the chest and upper abdominals.

STRAIGHT-LEG DEAD LIFT

1. In this variation of the dead lift, your legs remain nearly straight, but not immobile, throughout the movement. Your back will be more rounded than if you were performing regular dead lifts.
2. In a shoulder-width stance, hinge forward from the hips until your chest is parallel with the floor. Your legs and hips should move back and forth as you are lifting the weight, but no vertical movement of the legs should occur through bending of the knees.

Arms and Shoulders

Every exercise included in this book has been selected for the purpose of enhancing postural stabilization and improving sport proficiency for triathletes. Arm and shoulder strength contribute significantly toward attaining and supporting this goal. The triathlete will find the following exercises exceptionally beneficial for improving and sustaining optimal posture for swimming, cycling, and running.

FIVE-WAY EXERCISE BAND ARM TRAINER

Tie an elastic cord or exercise band around a pole or thread it through an eye hook or carabiner at shoulder height. Standing, perform the following exercises in sequence for 15 to 20 repetitions or for 30-second time increments for 3 sets. Advanced athletes may use a disk pillow and the march position.

1. External fly: Facing the pole or wall and with your arms to the front grasping the band, externally rotate both arms until they are in line with your shoulders (a).

a

2. Medial rotation: With your back toward the pole or wall bend both arms in right angles with your lower arms, rotate your arms downward (medially) toward the floor.

3. External rotation: Facing the pole or wall and with your elbows up and your forearms and palms down, externally rotate your hands and forearms toward the ceiling (b).

4. Internal reverse fly: With your back toward the pole or wall and your arms held out at shoulder height, bring your hands together in front of you (c).

5. Down-insweep: Stand on the right leg as you face the pole or wall with your right arm extended holding the cord. Pull the cord down and in toward your chest.

b

c

UPRIGHT ROW-HANG CLEAN

1. Take a shoulder-width grip on the bar.
2. Standing, clean the weight to thigh height.
3. Lift the barbell up to chest height, leading with your elbows.
4. Return the barbell to thigh height and repeat.

SHOULDER SHRUG

1. Standing with your feet shoulder-width apart, take a barbell or two dumbbells in your hands.
2. Elevate your shoulders toward your ears while maintaining a straight back.
3. Now rotate your shoulders backward.

SINGLE-LEGGED STANDING BICEPS CURL

1. Stand with your back erect, your knees slightly flexed, and your feet shoulder-width apart.
2. Hold a dumbbell in each hand with your palm facing inward and your thumbs forward.
3. Bring one knee into the march position (knee up, thigh parallel to floor). As an option, you may stand on a disk pillow.
4. Alternate curling your arms upward one at a time, rotating your palm so it faces your shoulder.
5. Do an equal number of repetitions with the right and left legs raised.

SEATED BICEPS CURL TO REVERSE OVERHEAD PRESS

1. Sit on a stability ball while holding a dumbbell in each hand at your sides with your thumbs forward.
2. Curl both biceps at the same time, rotating your palms toward your shoulders.
3. Press the weights overhead with your palms facing inward and the backs of your wrists facing out.
4. At the top of the press, rotate your palms outward, return the dumbbells to your shoulders, and reverse the curl to the starting position.

TRICEPS PRESS-DOWN

1. Using a cable or exercise bands, start with your elbows at your sides and both hands flexed at chest height.
2. Press your forearms down until your arms are at full extension. To simulate the freestyle swimming pull, open your hands from the beginning through the end of the press.
3. Hold for one second and return.
4. Repeat.

LYING TRICEPS EXTENSION

1. Lie on your back with a stability ball positioned beneath your shoulder blades.
2. Hold a barbell or two dumbbells with your hands four to six inches apart.
3. Raise the weight straight above your chest.
4. Lower the weights by flexing your forearms toward your shoulders.
5. Extend your arms to the starting position and repeat.

The Lower Body

The lower-body exercises that follow strengthen the primary lower-body muscle groups that power swimming, cycling, and running movements. The supplemental training program for these muscles ensures that adequate strength is gained for these movements and averts muscle imbalances to improve performance.

SINGLE-LEGGED WALL SQUAT

1. Place a stability ball between your lower back and a wall.
2. Bring one of your knees to the march position, then cross it over the other knee or extend the leg out front.
3. Squat slowly, with the center of the knee tracking always over the second toe.
4. Try the same movement holding a medicine ball overhead or away from your chest, or with dumbbells or a barbell on your shoulders.

SINGLE-LEGGED PROPRIOCEPTION SQUAT

1. Stand with one leg on a disk pillow and the other leg in the march position.
2. Slowly squat four to six inches, maintaining core stabilization by drawing in the abdominal muscles.
3. Do 10 to 15 repetitions on each leg.
4. Advance this exercise by holding the dumbbells overhead, in the curl-up position, or at your sides. Other ways to make this exercise more complex are to complete it without a disk pillow, holding the dumbbells at the hip-in curl-up position, squatting and curling both arms simultaneously, and performing a reverse press overhead from the curl position.

LUNGE COMPLEX

1. Lunge slowly forward with one leg.
2. Keep your back straight, chest up, chin level, and eyes looking forward while you contract the abdominals.
3. Slowly bring your rear leg forward into the march position (with your knee up and your thigh parallel to the floor).
4. Hold for five seconds, drawing in the transversus abdominis again.
5. Next, extend and lunge forward.
6. Make four reverse (backward) lunges with the same leg.
7. Return to the march position and repeat with the other leg.
8. Also try this exercise while holding a medicine ball overhead or away from your chest, or use a weighted bar resting on your shoulders or dumbbells held either at your sides or overhead.

STABILITY BALL HAMSTRING CURL

1. Lie on your back on the floor and place your heels on top of a stability ball.

2. Bridge up to lift your hips off the floor so that you are resting on your shoulders.

3. Bring your heels (still on the ball) toward your buttocks and then return to the start position.

4. You can also perform these curls with only one leg on the ball at a time. As shown the noncurling leg is held high above the ball.

HANG-CLEAN-PUSH-PRESS TO FRONT LUNGE SQUAT

1. Grip a barbell with your hands shoulder-width apart.

2. Stand with the bar at midthigh level.

3. With your back straight and chest up, squeeze together your shoulder blades and rotate your elbows outward.

4. Hinge forward slightly, letting the weight hang just above your knees (a). Your body weight should be on your heels (check this by wiggling your toes).

5. Take a deep breath and hold until lift is completed. Pull up, leading with the elbows and rising onto your toes until the weight is near chin height (b).

6. Bend your knees to drop down a couple of inches and catch the weight as you press it overhead (c).

7. Exhale.

8. Return the weight to your chest with your elbows pointing away from your body.

9. Lunge forward on one leg, keeping your back straight and chest high (d), and then come up.

a

b

c

d

VMO (VASTUS MEDIALIS OBLIQUE) SQUAT

1. Standing in an athletic posture (knees flexed, back straight, chest up, and chin up), hold a medicine ball at chest height. Alternatively, the medicine ball can be held overhead, under the legs, with one arm, or in other positions. You may also stand with each foot on a disk pillow.

2. Squat down until your thighs are parallel with the floor. Hold this position for 10 to 20 seconds.

3. Next, move up and down two to three inches for 10 to 15 repetitions.

SPLIT SQUAT JUMP WITH MEDICINE BALL TOSS

1. Standing, hold a medicine ball in both hands as they rest on your right upper thigh.
2. Lunge forward with your left leg.
3. Now, swing the right thigh and leg forward and upward vigorously, tossing the medicine ball during the forward swing.
4. Next, lunge on the right leg, squat and jump up, and return to the squat.
5. Repeat, beginning with the medicine ball on the other leg.

SINGLE-LEGGED STEP BOX

1. Place a step box (8 to 24 inches high) against a wall.
2. Hold a medicine ball above your head and step onto the box with your left foot (a).
3. Step up forcefully, tapping the medicine ball against the wall. Your foot should rise off the step box momentarily while you touch the highest possible point with the ball (b).
4. Do 10 to 15 repetitions with the right leg, then repeat with the left leg.

a   b

JUMP MEDICINE BALL PICK-UP

1. Standing, place a medicine ball between your ankles.
2. Make a shallow squat down.
3. Explosively lift the ball up by jumping upward (pull your knees up).
4. Catch the ball and repeat for the repetitions indicated in the training phase.

PLYOMETRIC FOOT AGILITY

1. Make a 2-foot cross on the floor with tape.
2. Standing next to the tape, hop sideways over the tape on both legs 10 times, springing off your feet as quickly as possible. Once your feet hit the ground on the other side, you should begin the next hop.
3. Hop forward and backward over the tape 10 times, again springing back immediately after landing.
4. Hop diagonally first to the right and then to the left over the tape 10 times, springing back at each landing.
5. Do one round on both legs and then a second on one leg.

Using Supplemental Training in Your Program

Undeniably, every sport requires a measure of endurance, strength, and power, but the differentiating characteristics of sport performance determine how a supplemental training program is developed for that sport. Triathletes have different muscle needs than do, say, 350-pound NFL linemen; triathletes' strength requirements are for long endurance competitions requiring high-intensity repetitive contractions at or near the anaerobic threshold.

Athletes perform supplemental dryland training to enhance performance, avoid injury, rehabilitate, and develop strength, power, endurance, and flexibility. This training, however, should not interfere with the development of swimming, cycling, and running skills. Rather, the purpose is to enhance performance and therefore, in most circumstances, supplemental training should follow sport-specific training. Supplemental dryland training is essentially intended to promote functional capacity and stabilization. These characteristics are at the very heart of why augmenting triathlon training with supplemental dryland exercise is so important.

I integrate supplemental dryland training into my triathletes' periodized programs, presented in part II of this book, by using five phases (called A, B, C, D, and E) of dryland training. Each phase consists of variable exercises and different sets and repetitions, intensities and rhythms, and rest periods to correspond with the training periodization for swimming, biking, and running training. For example, phase E is applied to restoration and recovery periods, while phase A is used during base preparation training.

Dryland training, like swimming-, cycling-, and running-specific training, follows a strategy to achieve the best possible fitness at the right time. Table 5.1 summarizes which exercises are appropriate for each dryland phase, while table 5.2 provides the sets, repetitions, and methods that are appropriate for each period.

Table 5.1 Supplemental Dryland Training Exercises and Phases

Abdominal core exercises	Phase A	Phase B	Phase C	Phase D	Phase E
V-Up and Over	✓	✓			
Quadriplex Contralateral Extension	✓	✓			✓
Back Extension	✓		✓		
Stability Ball Crunch	✓	✓	✓	✓	
Pelvic Roll-Up			✓		✓
Hanging Leg Raise with Medicine Ball	✓	✓	✓		
Isolateral Flexion and Extension	✓	✓		✓	✓
Prone Bridge	✓	✓	✓	✓	
Single-Armed Ball Bridge	✓		✓		✓
Five-Way Rollout Series	✓	✓			
Single-Legged Step Box Stability Ball Rollout	✓	✓			
Transversus Abdominis		✓			✓
Chest and back	Phase A	Phase B	Phase C	Phase D	Phase E
Stability Ball Inclined Push-Up	✓			✓	
Three-Way Stability and Medicine Ball Push-Up		✓	✓		
Disk and Tubing Lateral Fly	✓			✓	
Stability Ball "Bench" Press	✓		✓		
Stability Ball Flexed-Arm Pullover		✓			✓
Incline Stability Ball Dumbbell Fly or Press-Up			✓		
Front Lateral Pull-Down	✓	✓		✓	✓
Cable Lateral Extension	✓		✓		

Chest and back *(continued)*	Phase A	Phase B	Phase C	Phase D	Phase E
Seated Pulley Row	✓	✓			✓
Straight-Leg Dead Lift	✓	✓			
Arms and shoulders	Phase A	Phase B	Phase C	Phase D	Phase E
Five-Way Exercise Band Arm Trainer	✓	✓	✓	✓	✓
Upright Row-Hang Clean	✓	✓			
Shoulder Shrug	✓				
Single-Legged Standing Biceps Curl	✓		✓		
Seated Biceps Curl to Reverse Overhead Press		✓		✓	✓
Triceps Press-Down		✓	✓		
Lying Triceps Extension		✓			
Lower body	Phase A	Phase B	Phase C	Phase D	Phase E
Single-Legged Wall Squat	✓	✓			
Single-Legged Proprioception Squat	✓			✓	
Lunge Complex	✓		✓		
Stability Ball Hamstring Curl	✓	✓	✓	✓	✓
Hang-Clean-Push-Press to Front Lunge Squat	✓	✓			
VMO (Vastus Medialis Oblique) Squat	✓	✓	✓		
Split Squat Jump with Medicine Ball Toss	✓				
Single-Legged Step Box		✓	✓		
Jump Medicine Ball Pick-Up	✓		✓		
Plyometric Foot Agility	✓	✓	✓	✓	✓

Table 5.2   Supplemental Dryland Training Phases

Phase	Purpose	% of One Rep Maximum (1RM)	Reps per Set	Rhythm of Lift	Rest Intervals	Sets	Method
A	Muscular endurance/ reps	40–60%	15–20	Fast	10–30 sec between reps; 1 min between sets	1–3	1 × 20 1 × 15 1 × 15
A	Muscular endurance/ time	40–60%	30 sec	Fast	5–10 sec between reps; 30–60 sec between sets	1–3	Circuit training; move from one exercise to the next
B	Power/ maximum strength	75–80%	10–12	Moderate	1 min or no rest interval if complex circuit (such as Olympic platform combina- tion lifts)	3–4	1 × 10 1 × 12 1 × 10 1 × 12
C	Explosive power	80–90%	6–10	Explosive	1–2 min	2–3	1 × 10 1 × 8 1 × 6
D	Maximum strength	90–100%	2–6	Slow	2+ min	2–4	1 × 6 1 × 4 1 × 3 1 × 2
E	Restoration and recovery	30–40%	15–20	Moderate	No rest interval	1	Circuit training; move from one exercise to the next

As you delve into part II of the book, you'll see how each phase presented here fits into a comprehensive, periodized training program for triathletes.

YOUR TRAINING PROGRAM

CHAPTER 6

Training With Intensity

As a triathlete begins conditioning, metabolic and physical adaptations occur as a result of training overload. Conversely, inactivity for an endurance athlete reduces aerobic capacity fairly quickly. A training program and the workouts it is composed of provide the structure for training in the form of progression of intensity and volume as well as specificity, while individual differences in athletes also determine the outcome. All of this occurs as a result of the type of activity, intensity, duration of workouts, speed, restoration, and frequency of training and competitions.

This process of conditioning highlights the five principles of training successfully.

Overload indicates that the musculoskeletal, cardiopulmonary, and metabolic systems must be exercised beyond the accustomed level for training effects to take place.

Reversibility indicates that if training overload is discontinued, improvements will be lost. The adage "use it or lose it" is definitive in this instance. While the amount of loss is difficult to determine, to minimize losses of fitness, athletes are best off if they sustain fitness as much as possible even when taking restoration breaks from training. To do so means to swim, bike, and run at lower intensity levels and less often, but not to stop altogether.

Specificity in training indicates that the training effects are most significant when the specific energy systems (intensity) and specific practices (neuromuscular development) needed to perform in competition are trained. In basic terms, swimming, biking, and running develop movement patterns that lend themselves to increased motor skills in swimming, biking, and running, respectively.

Progression refers to how the overload is applied over time to achieve optimal adaptation and improvements in fitness.

Individual differences specify that training is more effective when planned specifically for an individual and his or her level of experience, competition goals, relative fitness, age, gender, and amount of personal time available for training. The longer I coach, the more I recognize the importance of paying attention to the individual needs of each athlete. Certainly there are similarities in exercises, drills, and training intensities, but the ingredients of each workout need to be tailored to the individual needs of the triathlete.

How training intensities coalesce with the principles of training is as much art as science. Yet, the foundation of most training programs is centered on training predominant energy systems of the body according to how these are optimally used for differing types of athletic competition. Different training intensities train the different energy systems. To successfully apply the principles of training, the program and workouts follow well-defined ranges of intensity. Intensity is the primary means of determining effort and is completely independent for each triathlete.

An Olympic lift, a baseball swing, a tennis serve, or a shot put throw are activities that predominately use strength and power (the nonoxidative energy system). These are all activities that require short bursts of power lasting under four seconds. At the other end of the spectrum, the triathlete relies more on aerobic endurance (the aerobic-oxidative system) for her event, which lasts from 1 to 17 hours.

Training Intensity Zones

Triathlon perhaps more than any other sport necessitates the use of the widest variety of training intensities. To that end, this chapter describes four training zones and subzones triathletes will use in this program. These zones are delineated by the degree of intensity, duration, targeted heart rate (HR), perceived exertion, workout characteristics, and work:rest ratio appropriate for each. Beginning in this chapter and continuing through chapter 9, you will see the best balance for each of these intensity zones according to which training phase you are in.

In determining the physiological benefits of each training zone, Jaci L. VanHeest, PhD, former director of exercise physiology for USA Swimming, has been helpful in providing references for each of the physiological and biological training benefits described in each training zone. I've provided these references in the reference list at the end of the book. Using the work of David E. Martin and Peter N. Coe, I have adapted and expanded several subsets to the following five conditioning training categories:

1. Recovery training
2. Aerobic conditioning
3. Anaerobic conditioning

4. Aerobic capacity

5. Anaerobic capacity

Each of these training intensities produces certain adaptations in the body that may not be duplicated at a higher or lower intensity—that is, the adaptation can only be achieved by training within that zone. For instance, zone 1 (aerobic conditioning) greatly improves the aerobic system and stimulates the formation of more capillaries in the muscles to enable oxygen-rich blood to be carried to more of the working muscles. Higher intensity training, such as zone 4 (anaerobic capacity), is almost the inverse of zone 1, stimulating anaerobic training and producing maximum lactate.

It is important to understand the physiology and training purpose of each zone and to learn how to work the right mixture of training in each zone into your workout program to produce optimal results. The program I provide throughout the rest of the book identifies and organizes each zone appropriately into a periodized training schedule based on four training phases: base preparation (chapter 6), base transition (chapter 7), race preparation (chapter 8), and peak transition (chapter 9).

© Empics

Training at the right intensity for the time of year will ensure that your body is ready to meet the demands of your race.

The following section details each training zone and its workout durations, HR targets, perceived exertion and workout characteristics for swimming, cycling, and running. Table 6.1 provides workout examples.

Table 6.1   Training Intensity Categories

	Recovery	Zone 1 (O₂)	Zone 2a (LVT-a)	Zone 2b (LVT-b)	Zone 2c (LVT-c)	Zone 3 (VO₂)	Zone 4 (LAC)
Workout Duration (min)	1–60	20–360	20–60	15–60	10–25	8–21	4–10
% Maximal HR	60–70	70–75	75–80	80–92	90–95	95–100	100+
RPE	Very, very light	Fairly light to somewhat hard	Somewhat hard	Hard	Harder	Very hard	Very, very hard
Details	Race and interval recovery	Aerobic conditioning	Sub-threshold development training	Race-pace threshold (Olympic triathlon pace)	Supra-threshold cruise intervals	High-intensity $\dot{V}O_2$ max aerobic capacity training	Speed, lactate tolerance, neurological development
Work: Rest	N/A	N/A	Short rest	Short rest	2:1	1:1	1:2 to 1:3
Swimming	500–1,000 m; long, easy strokes	Warm-ups, technique drills, kicking, pull sets	2–5 × 500 m, 30–60 sec rest	20–40 × 100 m, 5–10 sec rest; hard and hold even splits	8–20 × 100 m, 45 sec rest	2–6 × 200 m in 3 min, 3 min rest	5–20 × 25 m in 13 sec every 45 sec
Cycling	15–20 min high-rpm spinning	1–3+ h continuous, steady state	High-rpm spinning over varied terrain	15–40K time trial	3–5 × 5 min, 1 min rest, slightly above 40K race pace on roller or trainer	2–5 × 4 min, 4 min rest	6–18 × 20 min, 1 min rest
Running	12–20 min jog on soft surface	30–120+ min continuous trail running	20–60 min of low threshold running on flat to rolling terrain	3–7 × 1 mile hard, 1 min rest; hold or descend pace	Fartlek 2–6 × 4 min, 1 min rest; just under 10K race pace	2–6 × 800 m in 2:50, 2:50 rest	2–6 × 200 m in 40 sec, 80 sec rest

Recovery

Recovery training workouts unwind the intensity of higher levels of effort. They ease the body and loosen the muscles following intervals or stimulate recovery. In the days following a competition, recovery workouts act like a massage by gently encouraging blood flow and increasing muscle temperature to accelerate recuperation, and it quite simply feels good to move the muscles and allow the mind to reflect on the past race.

Following a hard track interval, swim set, or hill climb on the bike, a recovery period provides just the right stimulus to flush out and stretch the muscles. Recovery workouts are characterized by very, very light perceived exertion (RPE) and HRs as low as 60 percent of the maximum heart rate. Short, gentle swimming, cycling, and running workouts (lasting perhaps as little as 12 minutes of running to 30 minutes of cycling to 10 to 20 minutes of swimming) are sufficient as a recovery workout.

Aerobic Conditioning

The highest training volume triathletes do is in the aerobic conditioning zone (O_2). Except for recovery training, this training category is of the lowest intensity. Athletes cannot afford to dismiss this vital training intensity because it provides the physiological foundations that enable the body to handle the higher intensities as the competitive phases approach. This zone is essential in developing overall training progression and adaptation for optimal performance.

The duration of workouts in this zone can be anywhere from 20 minutes to several hours depending on the phase of training and competitive goal distances. HRs within this zone range from 70 to 75 percent of maximum and RPE can be characterized as "fairly light to somewhat hard."

There are many tangible physiological benefits of aerobic conditioning:

- It strengthens connective tissue (ligaments and tendons).
- Supporting muscles gain endurance capacity.
- It increases resistance to muscle cell damage.
- It causes slow-twitch muscle fibers to gain size and strength.
- It effectively stimulates motor neurons that contribute to improving exercise economy.
- It increases blood volume, allowing the blood to carry more hemoglobin (the oxygen-carrying molecules) to the working muscles.
- It generates a larger capacity for storage of muscle glycogen reserves (carbohydrates and water).
- It increases capillary development. Capillaries, the smallest blood vessels, are where oxygen is passed from the blood to the working muscles. Training increases the number of capillaries surrounding each muscle fiber, thus expanding the aerobic capacity of the triathlete.

- It increases the density of mitochondrial structures within muscle cells that produce ATP (adenosine triphosphate), an energy-rich compound that breaks down food in small amounts for use as energy.
- It reduces resting heart rate.
- It increases stroke volume (amount of blood pumped for each contraction of the heart).
- It improves temperature regulation and heat tolerance within the circulatory system.
- It increases respiratory endurance (lung ventilation).
- It improves free fatty acid (FFA) oxidation, sparing muscle glycogen (carbohydrate.) This means that this training helps the body become conditioned to using fats as energy before using carbohydrate reserves at lower intensities of exertion. The overall result is that more energy is reserved for later use and thus endurance is increased.
- It increases muscle glycogen storage capacity.
- It decreases body fat by inducing hormonal changes that enhance fat utilization and by requiring submaximal endurance training, which metabolically uses a lot of energy.

Anaerobic Conditioning

For the triathlete, having the ability to stave off high concentrations of lactic acid in the muscles as speed increases is precisely what improves performance. Anaerobic conditioning, also known as threshold training or lactate ventilatory threshold training (LVT), is the training zone that will improve this capacity most effectively.

The benefits of anaerobic conditioning include the following:

- It improves exercise economy, biomechanics and form, race speed, neuromuscular coordination, and aerobic capacity by recruiting specific muscles and developing lung capacity at or near race-pace efforts. Over many seasons of training, triathletes may not increase oxygen capacity much beyond the first season or two, but can improve performance by improving the economy of their movements (technique).
- It increases mitochondrial structures in the muscles. A greater supply of and larger mitochondria contribute significantly to prolonging sustained endurance performance.
- It increases myoglobin content; this boosts the oxygen capacity in muscles and helps transfer oxygen to the mitochondria.
- It increases the lactate threshold because trained triathletes have an increased aerobic capacity and improved rate of lactic acid removal.

- It enhances glycogen storage capacity.
- It increases race-specific neuromuscular movement by improving the efficiency of muscle cell recruitment. Better central nervous system to muscle coordination and stimulation is the result.
- It increases stamina.
- Slow- and fast-twitch fiber types remain unchanged, but metabolic capacities in fibers increase with training.
- It increases blood volume due to increases in plasma and hemoglobin volumes.

There are three sublevels of intensity that qualify as anaerobic conditioning. The first level is just below threshold for tempo training (LVT-a). The next is at threshold (LVT-b) for race-pace conditioning. And the last is just above threshold (LVT-c) for "cruise interval" training. The purpose and benefits of each subzone are described in the following sections and table 6.1.

LVT-a

"Tempo" is an effective word to describe this intensity zone. The training is rhythmic, balanced, and uninterrupted. HRs reach 75 to 80 percent of the maximal heart rate and RPE is at "somewhat hard." There is enough threshold development, but the training is not so demanding that the athlete cannot recover promptly for the next training session. For triathlon training, I believe this subzone is essential in balancing the progression of training.

LVT-a workout sets last 20 to 60 minutes and include short rest intervals. These are generally part of a combined intensity zone workout for swimming, biking, and running and are completed at a moderate intensity. Table 6.1 provides a few workout examples for this zone of training.

LVT-b

LVT-b training is defined as the intensity applied in an Olympic-distance triathlon race, time trial, or best effort. HRs range from 80 to 92 percent of the maximal heart rate and RPE is "hard." This is commonly referred to as the aerobic threshold or lactate threshold. Whichever is used, it is the pace at which a triathlete can hold maximal exertion without going "overboard" into oxygen debt and increasing lactic acid beyond his capacity for a sufficient removal rate. If you push too far or too hard, the burn you feel in your legs or arms will jolt your system down to a snail's pace.

LVT-b segments of workouts last 15 to 60 minutes and are often time trials or longer duration intervals with short rests (table 6.1). Over the course of a season, it's a good idea to gradually progress through these workout intensities rather than going all-out every time. For example, once you establish your time trial benchmarks, the next time you do a workout of LVT-b intensity, try improving by seconds rather than minutes.

LVT-c

LVT-c intensity is just above threshold (LVT-b) and is referred to as "cruise" pace or suprathreshold interval pace. For running, this pace is slightly faster than your typical pace for a 10K race. For cycling, it is a bit faster than the pace you believe you could hold to for 20 to 40K, and for swimming, it is your fastest 100 pace minus two seconds. With an RPE of "harder" and an HR of 90 to 95 percent of the maximal heart rate, this intensity zone provides another level of training above the threshold, but below aerobic capacity ($\dot{V}O_2$max).

LVT-c workouts are 10 to 25 minutes in duration and are performed in intervals such as swimming 8 × 100 m in 90 seconds with 45 seconds between intervals or running 8 × 400 m in 90 seconds with 45 seconds rest between intervals (work/rest ratio of 2:1).

Aerobic Capacity

Aerobic capacity ($\dot{V}O_2$) training intensity is the most demanding because the intensity is high and the duration is somewhat long. HRs are 95 to almost 100 percent of maximal heart rate and RPE is "very hard." The swimming intensity is equivalent to a 500 m time trial; the running intensity is that of a 5K race pace. For all intents and purposes, the triathlete is attempting to push just above the redline threshold for the entire distance, so efforts at this intensity cannot be made for too long in terms of time or distance. Rest intervals need to be equal to interval times or distances. Also, repetition intervals are from 2 to 8 minutes in length with the total volume of any workout being no more than 15 to 21 minutes at this level.

The benefits of aerobic capacity training include the following:

- It improves neuromuscular coordination because certain neurons have high energy thresholds; that is, those muscle fibers are recruited at higher intensities.
- It increases blood buffering (acid balance).
- It increases aerobic capacity up to the maximum value (which is genetically determined).
- It enhances glycogen storage and capacity.
- It increases muscular strength.

Anaerobic Capacity

Anaerobic capacity training (LAC) is high-intensity, short-duration training. HRs may reach approximately 100 percent, with an RPE characterized as "very, very hard." Speed, lactate tolerance, and neurological development are the chief benefits. For the triathlete, these sprint intervals, when combined with the extensive endurance work, are the icing on the cake.

LAC workout segments are 4 to 10 minutes long with a work:rest ratio of 1:2 to 1:3. A five-minute LAC swimming workout might be something like 8 × 50 m in 40 seconds with 80 seconds rest. A cycling workout may be something like 5 × 1 minute with 3 minutes rest; a running workout could be 10 × 30 seconds with 1 minute rest. The build up in intensity for the first several seconds of these intervals is quite high. Triathletes like doing these intervals because they get a great feeling of speed after doing the tremendous amounts of endurance work.

The benefits of anaerobic capacity training include the following:

- It increases neurological recruitment, power, strength, and coordination.
- It increases slow- and fast-twitch muscle fiber contractibility.
- Enzymes change to increase ATP-PC (adenosine triphosphate-phosphocreatine) conversion.
- It increases glycolytic ability (supply of ATP for muscular effort).
- It improves and increases blood buffering.
- It maximizes lactate tolerance (acidosis). Acidosis increases unbuffered acids in the blood or reduces the capacity for removing lactate.

Determining Training Intensity

The two most practical methods of determining training intensity are RPE and HR. Although neither is an absolute indicator of intensity, together these methods can help triathletes ensure that they are targeting the right intensity.

Using a Heart Rate Monitor

Many athletes see monitoring their heart rate as an absolute measure for determining their exercise intensity. However, heart rate is not as objective as we would all like it to be. Yes, as work (intensity) rates increase, oxygen consumption rises linearly, at least until maximal effort is approached. Heart rate therefore seems to be an accurate measure of intensity, and in many instances it is. But a caveat is that HR monitors themselves can have an error of 5 to 15 beats per minute.

Furthermore, many studies show that HR responses fluctuate due to variables like training, sleep status, stress, dehydration, weather, illness, and cardiac drift (see table 6.2). Cardiac drift—which occurs normally while you work at a constant load and appears to result from dehydration and the subsequent increase in muscle temperature—for example, can cause the HR to increase as much as 20 beats per minute. Thus, an athlete who tries to maintain a specific heart rate will need to constantly lessen effort and intensity rather than achieving the intensity that the workout calls for. So trying to

Table 6.2   Heart Rate Monitor Training Pros and Cons

HR Monitor Advantages	HR Monitor Disadvantages
Monitors overtraining markers Helps triathletes learn to identify training intensities Ideal for testing benchmarks with RPE	Inaccuracies due to • cardiac drift, which can raise HR 20 beats per minute • fluctuation in HR monitor display • environmental effects on HR • dehydration increases HR Need for frequent sport-specific testing of maximal HR to apply correct training zones

lock into a prescribed set of numbers on the readout can be misleading if HR is the only measure of intensity you are using.

Many triathletes I have worked with have had little experience using the Karvonen method to help them determine training HRs. Keep in mind that the Karvonen method and other nonlaboratory HR-determining formulas are estimates and do not provide the accuracy of metabolic testing done in a laboratory. However, the Karvonen method is calculated as a percentage of heart rate reserve (HRR)—the difference between your resting HR and maximum HR (HRmax)—and therefore tends to be more accurate than the old standby equation of 220 – age. The Karvonen method requires regular assessment of morning HR to apply the appropriate training HR levels. This is an excellent benefit since a morning HR provides a better indicator of over-training than do other HR assessments.

Perhaps most importantly, HRmax's are different for every sport. It is important, therefore, to test these periodically, as I describe in chapter 7. HRmax's are influenced by body position, muscle mass exercised, time of day, fitness and experience, method of contraction, topographical conditions, fluid level, and temperature.

In swimming, peak HRs are limited by cool water, the horizontal body position, and primarily using the upper body to generate movement. While cycling, the fact that the body weight is supported, wind, and the general predominance of the lower-body muscles for generating power make for a lower HRmax than, say, cross-country skiing, where the upper- and lower-body muscles are used. In running, impact forces, body weight, and the continuum of leg and upper-body movements generate the highest HRmax's for most triathletes. These activity-related differences are reflected in table 6.3.

When testing for HRmax and using HR as the indicator of exercise intensity, it is very important to consider the time of day, temperature, fitness level, fatigue from other workouts, personal motivation, and activity. At more than 70 degrees Fahrenheit (21 degrees Celsius), submaximal HRs rise about a beat per

Table 6.3   Modified Karvonen Heart Rate Table

Training Intensity Zone	O$_2$	LVT-a	LVT-b	LVT-c	VO$_2$	LAC
% Maximum Heart Rate	70	75	80	92	95	98

Enter your maximum values and calculate based on these percentages for each zone.

	Heart Rate					
Swimming maximum						
Biking maximum						
Running maximum						
Resting						

Also find your heart rate reserves by subtracting resting heart rate from your maximum heart rates.

HR reserve swimming: _____   HR reserve biking: _____   HR reserve running: _____

Example:

Training Intensity Zone	O$_2$	LVT-a	LVT-b	LVT-c	VO$_2$	LAC
% Maximum Heart Rate	70	75	80	92	95	98
Heart Rate						
Swimming maximum	180	138	145	152	169	173	177
Biking maximum	172	132	139	146	161	165	169
Running maximum	185	142	149	156	173	178	182
Resting	40						

HR reserve swimming: __*140*__   HR reserve biking: __*132*__   HR reserve running: __*145*__ minute for each degree of temperature increase. Therefore, if you test HR for the run on a cool morning and for the bike segment at midday when it's humid and sunny, the results could very well be misleading: the bike HR could peak closer to the run HR as a result of the higher air temperature, but in a more objective setting, there might be 10 heart beats' difference. It's common for many geographic areas to see such humidity variations from morning to afternoon.

Training effectively with an HR monitor is not as simple as estimating your target HRs and happily training away as you read your watch. As I pointed out, a large number of variables can affect HR during exercise. However, to be more accurate, using a HR monitor along with the Karvonen method helps reduce the inconsistencies of training just with HR. Of course, I always have the triathletes I work with pay very close attention to their RPE, as well.

HR monitoring when used with the Karvonen method is an effective tool for testing and determining if an athlete is suffering from overtraining (see sidebar below). Overtraining can reduce fitness as a result of ongoing cardiac stress brought about by too much exercise (progression of volume, intensity, or frequency in exercise) without enough recovery to allow the body to rebuild and regenerate. The result of overtraining is a gradual decline in performance, and the muscles are heavy, illness is frequent, and emotions are out of sorts. The later indications of overtraining are anxiety, depression, anger, or irritability. None of these are good for triathletes.

Recognizing Overtraining by Measuring Heart Rate

With a sound training program, an athlete will not experience high levels of overtraining, if any. You can monitor your training to be sure to avoid overtraining in two ways that help fine-tune the training process.

1. First, take your resting pulse in the morning. This will help you take note of when training is too taxing, when it's on target, and even when it's improving, as evidenced by a reduced resting pulse rate.

2. Second, train with an HR monitor so you'll have objective data to match with RPE.

You should monitor your morning HR and psychological feelings (table 6.4) to check for signs and symptoms of overtraining. Psychological symptoms tend to precede an upward trend in the morning HR, which is a sure sign that you are overtraining your body.

To determine if you are overtraining, take your HR each morning before getting out of bed and also take notice of your psychological symptoms. When the trend line from one morning to another is upward by more than five beats, a change in training and increased rest are necessary.

Table 6.5 references other common signs and symptoms of overtraining, plus the treatment methods to use to overcome it and to avoid overtraining in the first place.

Table 6.4   Heart Rate Training and Monitoring Chart   Month _____

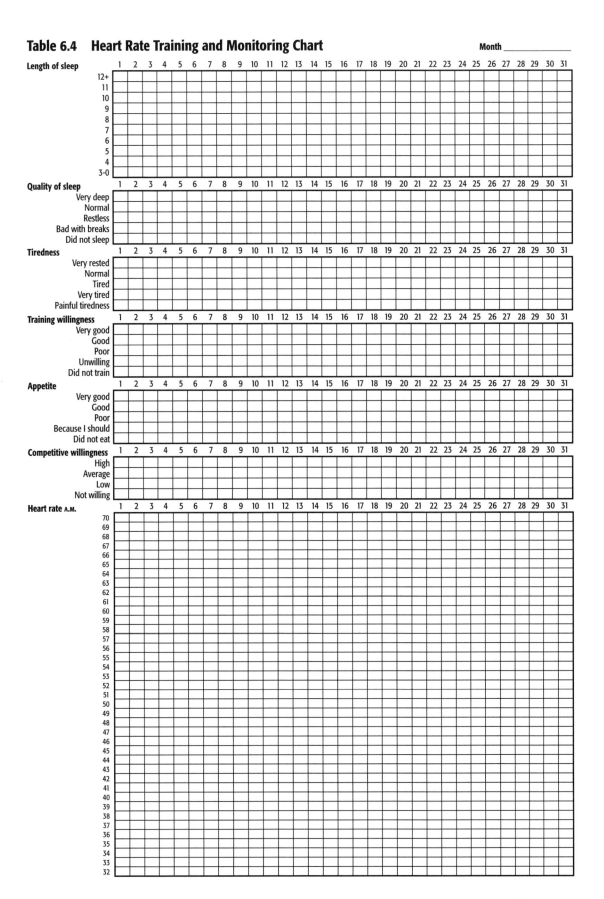

Table 6.5   Overtraining Symptoms and Treatments

Physical Symptom	Psychological Symptom	Treatment
High (>5 beats) morning heart rate for 2 or 3 consecutive days	Chronic fatigue	Rest
Weight loss	Anxiety	Nutrition
Increased body temperature	Drowsiness	Fluids
Low HR during training with high RPE	Poor concentration	Light exercise
Increased thirst	Irritability	Massage

Rating of Perceived Exertion

The rating of perceived exertion, or RPE (table 6.6), is considered to be too subjective a measuring tool, but it has proven to be remarkably accurate in helping athletes to understand intensity. With sufficient practice, I believe RPE to be the most reliable method of estimating effort, especially when it's used to validate the data received from an HR monitor.

By using a CompuTrainer and coaching software, block-shaped ramp tests can be repeated with great accuracy while measuring watts, peak watts, HR, RPE, and cadence in a fairly repeatable environment. That is, the workload and protocols are the same and therefore pretest training can be somewhat controlled. This, then, is a great way to use HR and RPE together to monitor improvements in fitness.

Table 6.6   RPE Scale

6	No exertion at all
7	
8	Extremely light
9	Very light
10	
11	Light
12	
13	Somewhat hard
14	
15	Hard (heavy)
16	
17	Very hard
18	
19	Extremely hard
20	Maximal exertion

Borg RPE scale
© Gunnar Borg, 1970, 1985, 1994, 1998

Periodizing Training Into Phases

Most coaches organize a season or multiple seasons of training into phases or blocks emphasizing different things, resulting in varied volumes of training, types of workouts, and testing components. I follow a similar approach; however, my program is distinguished by its organization of periodizing each training element. Not only are the training intensity, volume, and frequency varied, the components of dryland training, the number of swim, bike, and running workouts, the testing for each sport, and standard and specific workout targets for each week are also varied. The purpose of this is so that intensity, volume, and the training building blocks promote optimal periodization and progression in training.

In North America and to a large degree worldwide, the triathlete off-season typically begins with the completion of the Ironman Hawaii triathlon held every year in October and Olympic course world championships held around the same time. After the last major event of a lengthy and intense season, it is time for restoration and regeneration of the psyche and the physical body. During this four- to eight-week active rest, the triathlete reduces the volume, intensity, and frequency of training while taking pleasure in multiple cross training sports. Swimming, cycling, and running are included in active restoration too, but as low-intensity efforts and in unstructured workouts. When training begins in earnest again for the new season, the athlete should feel refreshed from the active rest and ready to refocus on goals for the upcoming season.

The base preparation training phase is what training begins with. This phase can last for up to 16 weeks. Technique, aerobic conditioning, flexibility, and slow volume buildup are the main focuses. It is during this time that triathletes establish the "base" on which the subsequent periods of training and successful competitions are built.

Base transition periodization is a four-week cycle of slightly more specific training, increasing volume, transition work, and gradually increasing training zone intensities. This phase predictably prepares the triathlete for the upcoming race preparation cycles.

During race preparation training, triathletes specifically prepare for competition with highly defined and targeted workouts. The training volume is lowered, but the intensity is driven upward in each intensity zone. Prior to most important competitions, the intensity is tapered during peak transition training.

During peak transition, the overall training volume of swimming, cycling, and running is reduced over 7 to 21 days (depending on the competition distance). The intensity of training and dryland intensity rise while the number of stretching sessions and rest days increase.

Chapters 7 through 10 look closely at each of these phases of training to show you how to organize, manage, and implement these cycles within your own programs.

Training Volume for the Season

A triathlete's training volume for each respective sport is determined by his competitive history, assessment (current fitness), goals, and athletic history. If you have little training history, it is prudent for your training volume to progress conservatively. In general, the key to any good training plan is that it be dynamic enough to accommodate constant changes in health, time, seasons, and even enthusiasm. Most triathletes compete at a variety of distances, including a combination of some sprint races, some Olympic-distance, some long-course, and some Ironman competitions, and this factor—what races a triathlete sees as being most significant—should also play a role in determining seasonal training volume.

The total program volume is the amount of time you intend to spend training over the season. This is likely determined by analyzing your previous years of training and the competition lengths for the upcoming season. Rob Sleamaker and Ray Browning's *Serious Training for Endurance Athletes* (Human Kinetics, 1996) is an excellent resource for determining your training volume based on your training level. In table 6.7, I've modified Sleamaker and Browning's categories to break down training hours by disciplines—swimming, cycling, and running. Athletes often come to the sport of triathlon with a background in one or two of the three sports, and it can be helpful to individualize training volumes to cater to a particular athlete's strengths and weaknesses. Table 6.7 provides guidelines for training volumes and time in swimming, cycling, and running for triathletes of calibers from world class and top amateur to good amateur, average amateur, and beginner.

I have found that surprisingly few elite professionals and competitive amateurs follow highly structured plans of training. Without a doubt, many achieve great results without much obvious organization in their training. A lot can be said for genetic talent, but I believe that to rise to one's individual best, planning and structure are necessary. Even so, training should be dynamic enough that structure doesn't completely dictate or override subjective feelings about the program (positively and negatively). In other words, a training program is merely a plan and how you feel physically and emotionally ultimately determine the course of action. This, perhaps, is what a coach primarily helps the athlete with when "coaching" is boiled down to its essence. As Scott Tinley used to tell me when I coached him, "It's not so much what you tell me to do, but what you tell me not to do." So, even as you plan your training, don't forget to take into account how you feel daily. Also, remember that joy comes from accomplishing goals that were obtained without sacrificing personal balance.

Table 6.7   Recommended Annual Training Volumes

	World Class		Top Amateur		Good Amateur		Average Amateur		Beginner	
	Volume (K)	Hours	Volume (K)	Hours	Volume (K)	Hours	Volume (K)	Hours	Volume (K)	Hours
Swimming										
Olympic	625	139	475	119	325	90	275	92	225	94
Half-Ironman	725	161	575	144	425	118	375	125	325	136
Ironman	825	183	675	169	525	146	475	158	425	177
Cycling										
Olympic	8,000	400	6,500	325	5,000	250	3,500	175	2,000	100
Half-Ironman	9,000	462	7,500	385	6,000	308	4,500	231	3,000	154
Ironman	10,500	583	9,000	500	7,500	417	6,000	333	4,500	250
Running										
Olympic	1,600	178	1,250	139	1,000	111	750	83	500	56
Half-Ironman	1,900	224	1,600	188	1,400	165	1,150	135	750	88
Ironman	2,300	288	2,000	250	1,800	225	1,400	175	1,000	125
Total										
Olympic		717		583		451		350		250
Half-Ironman		847		717		591		491		378
Ironman		1,054		919		788		666		552

Base Preparation Phase

The ability to compete at peak athletic levels depends first and foremost on the athlete's base preparation. A concentrated base is the foundation, core, and framework that best performances rely on. Base preparation includes exercising at low intensities for long durations—the building blocks used to construct the higher intensity efforts that come later. Dryland training (strength, core, flexibility) plays a chief role in base preparation training to comprehensively prepare the triathlete.

Too many triathletes want to get to the more intense work and neglect this important training. As I like to say, "The bigger the base, the better you'll race." Base training is the most important training and preparation part of the season.

As noted in chapter 6, the base preparation period of training picks up from active restoration and includes 16 weeks of foundational work in endurance, strength, flexibility, and technique. The general benefits of base preparation training include the following:

- Develops sport-specific aerobic endurance
- Develops strength, flexibility, neuromuscular coordination, and technique
- Strengthens connective tissue
- Increases the number of mitochondria and capillaries within the muscles
- Increases blood volume
- Enhances glycogen storage and capacity
- Decreases resting HR and increases stroke volume

These benefits are achieved by meeting the objectives of the phase, which include:

1. Assessing current fitness

2. Gradually increasing aerobic capacity and endurance (oxygen consumption)

3. Adding to core and maximal muscle strength

4. Progressively overloading and building up workout frequency, volume, and intensity

5. Promoting neurological development of proper technique patterns to improve economy

6. Training with drills to improve flexibility and coordination (technical exercises)

7. Managing nutrition and rest

8. Transitioning (aerobic/stamina) to bike-to-run workouts of longer duration and low intensity

Base preparation begins by assessing and establishing the athlete's current baseline fitness and from there establishing short-term, midrange, and long-range goals. I use a battery of pretests to determine an athlete's swimming, cycling, and running fitness. This is followed by another or several periodic retests to evaluate progress throughout this phase. These tests help define the direction of the training plan by establishing objective training benchmarks, which can be repeated over time. From these benchmarks, an athlete can better establish realistic goals that will give their training and racing a sense of purpose and direction.

Field Tests

Performance field tests are perhaps the best way to objectively measure training status. The tests must be repeatable and measurably accurate to provide an objective result. Later in this chapter, I present two pretests each for swimming, cycling, and running. Try to have two or three days of light training between assessment tests. Also try to replicate for each test the amount of rest you got before the prior test, the time of day you took the test, and the nutritional choices you made, and make sure to be well hydrated.

Do an ample warm-up of 15 to 25 minutes of easy effort along with several minutes of stretching before each test. The tests provide benchmarks for developing the training program and making an objective assessment of performance capacity in swimming, cycling, and running. During each test, note your efficiency during the trial; this will later help you determine whether technique, endurance, or both need attention in training.

Swimming Tests

The two swimming pretests that I recommend are equally effective, and I have no preference for using one over the other. The first method is the

500- to 1,650-yard (short course) time trial (400 to 1,500 m long course). Beginners and recreational triathletes will do fine with the shorter distances as benchmark tests, but experienced triathletes should test at the longer distance. The test is easy to administer, but nonetheless challenges the athlete to perform well. You'll first warm up and then swim the designated distance at your best-effort (LVT-b) pace. The time from this effort is used as the basis for developing the training objectives and program. The specifics of the test will be detailed later in the chapter.

The second test—and perhaps the more useful and interesting one for data lovers—is the graded swim test. In this protocol, you'll swim 8 × 200 yards or meters, leaving on a sendoff interval that is 2.5 times your predicted or actual best 200 time plus 10 seconds. For example, if your best 200 time is 2:30 (150 seconds), then the sendoff interval would be 2.5 × 150 seconds plus 10 seconds equals 385 seconds or 6:30 (rounded to nearest :30 seconds). The sendoff interval is used to maintain the same rest interval between each swim, thereby managing the actual swim time for each 200 during the test. The objective you're to try to meet is to swim each 200 yards 2 to 4 seconds faster with each repetition. Here's the step-by-step process:

1. Determine your best 200-yard or m swim time in seconds.

2. Multiply that time by 2.5 and add 10 seconds.

3. Using the modified Borg Scale of Perceived Exertion (see table 6.6 on page 136), complete the first swim at a level of effort that is fairly light. Do not swim the first 200 faster than this level of effort allows. A good guideline is to swim at least 30 seconds slower than your best 200 time plus 10 seconds.

4. Increase the intensity of each successive 200 by swimming one or two seconds faster per 100. The last 200 should be at an effort level of "very hard."

5. Have your coach or training partner record the time and stroke count during each swim. Time begins with your first movement, and 100-yard or m splits are to be recorded. Also record the stroke count for any of the 25 or 50 m following the first 50.

6. Record the time, HR, and RPE immediately after each swim. Your HR can be taken at the carotid artery at your neck or by a heart monitor reading. RPE is your perception of what the exertion felt like.

These data serve as an objective record of your aerobic and endurance fitness and establish a basis for measuring improvement throughout the season. Having the capacity to descend (decreasing the swim time) by controlling your swim times indicates that you have exceptional pace management and improving fitness. When you record swim time, sendoff interval, RPE, and HR, subsequent swim tests (done about every eight weeks) will objectively reveal any training development.

Cycling Tests

In general, it is more difficult to establish objective cycling benchmarks on the road because environmental, traffic, and other conditions affect the outcome of your ride. If you aren't able to find a suitably safe time-trial course on public roads, you may want to perform the cycling pretest on a trainer or rollers.

For a solid cycling pretest on the road, find a course 5, 10, or 15 miles in length over flat to rolling terrain, or find a hill climb of 3 to 5 miles with any range of grades. I prefer the hill time trial because I believe it to be a more objective estimate, and the shorter course offers less, if any, opportunity for interruption from the environment, traffic, and stop signs. Although some athletes are better climbers than others and this pretest may seem to favor them, remember that the purpose is to collect for an individual cyclist objective information that can be used to improve performance. The test protocol for the road time trial is:

1. Warm up with 20 to 30 minutes of aerobic conditioning pace (O_2) spinning. Be sure to drink at least eight ounces of cold fluids during the warm-up.

2. Establish the halfway or turnaround checkpoint on the course so that you can note your HR, RPE, and trail time at this point.

3. Maintain a constant best effort throughout the course with the goal of consistently staying at LVT-b pace.

4. On finishing, note your time, HR, and RPE.

With today's technology, just about anyone can take an indoor performance test. CompuTrainer, one of the world's leading home-use cycling ergometer and software products, makes training and testing performance even more functional by providing information on optimal bike fit and cadence, pedal analysis, SpinScan assessment (analysis of pedaling stroke), and, perhaps most important, a measure of the average watts (power) generated during testing.

For the most part, I use a block-shaped protocol for testing endurance athletes on the CompuTrainer. Actually, the system has preloaded protocols that you can select from, or you can design your own. Perhaps the most useful protocol is the five-minute, 50-watt block step-up protocol. This test begins with the athlete producing 100 watts and increases each five minutes by another 50. Here's how you can use this protocol:

1. Warm up for 15 minutes, generating 75 to 125 watts per stroke.

2. After the warm-up, calibrate your tire pressure to two pounds.

3. Begin the test by recording your beginning RPE.

4. Start pedaling at 100 watts for the first five minutes. The software program will raise the wattage by 50 watts every five minutes. Try to maintain 90 rpm; the test ends when your rpm falls to 70. Chart the

time, average watts, heart rate, RPE, and cadence at the end of each five-minute block.

5. Warm down for 10 to 15 minutes.

Again, tests should be performed about every eight weeks. HR, RPE, and average and peak watt values provide, for the most part, an objective measure of the progress and decline of performance.

Running Test

A reliable field test that I have used for some time for running is the Balke protocol. It's simple to execute and administer and provides objective information about running-specific fitness. The protocol also provides a formula for estimating running maximum oxygen-uptake capacity ($\dot{V}O_2$max), the laboratory-measured amount of oxygen you consume in one minute as you work at full capacity. By definition, $\dot{V}O_2$max is your maximal rate of oxygen consumption; it is a measure of your capacity to generate the energy required for endurance activities and is important in determining performance potential and assessing fitness improvements.

The protocol for the Balke Running $\dot{V}O_2$max Field Test is as follows:

1. Warm up for 15 to 20 minutes of light jogging on a 400 m track.

2. Stretch for 5 to 10 minutes.

3. During the test, run around the track for 15 minutes at an RPE of "hard to very hard" (LVT-b to LVT-c)

4. During the run, have your coach or the assistant record:

   • The total distance covered to the nearest 50 meters

   • The time of each 400 m segment, as well as your HR and RPE (call them out at the appropriate times)

   • The time, HR, and RPE at the end of the 15 minutes

Once the test is finished, you can estimate your $\dot{V}O_2$max using the following formula:

$$\text{Distance covered}/15 - 133 \times 0.172 + 33.3$$

So, for example,

for 4,000 m, the estimated $\dot{V}O_2$max is 56.3;

for 4,500 m, the estimated $\dot{V}O_2$max is 62.0; and

for 5,000 m, the estimated $\dot{V}O_2$max is 67.8.

This test not only estimates maximal oxygen capacity, it also provides very useful information on HR, RPE, and the distance covered. Even more important, it is a repeatable protocol that should be completed every eight weeks to determine the effects of training, monitor pace, and identify any modifications to the program that might be needed.

Workout Plan

Now that you have taken the pretests in each sport and assessed your functional strength (chapter 1), you are ready put together the essential components of the program, organize the periodization, and determine the number of swimming, biking, running, and supplemental training workouts to do in each week of this 16-week phase.

Periodization is about managing specific aspects of training, not just about controlling training volume and features. Rather, periodization works best with a wide-ranging assemblage of training variables that you can choose from to build your workouts.

I like to organize each training phase in its own workout table to provide an overview of the entire phase (see table 7.1). Along the top of the table are the starting date of the training week, what chronological training week it is (1, 2, 3, and so on), and what periodization phase is represented (for example, "BP16" is week 16, the first of the 16 weeks of base preparation).

Along the left-hand side of the table are the following categories, each used for swimming, cycling, and running:

Workouts (weekly). The recommended number of swimming, cycling, or running workouts for that week are based on your needs and your coach's observations. For example, if you're a beginning swimmer, you may need more base preparation workouts for technique than an experienced swimmer does.

Targets. Targets are training suggestions that add a "training relationship" to the phase of training by including specific elements in one or more workouts. The targets are primarily based on the phase of training and include intensity and skill training. Targets frequently reflect the results of coaching and musculoskeletal assessment findings. Targets should guide the program dynamically, initially being fitted to the phase of training and then being customized for each triathlete. Targets also indicate when the periodic tests are called for. Note that tests do not occur in the same weeks for swimming, cycling, and running. Specific workout targets are detailed on pages 154 to 160.

Transitions. This row notes the weeks that will include transition workouts (from the bike to running). While I do not specifically design swim-to-bike transition work, this is something that can be done as well. For many triathletes, Saturday morning swims are followed by cycling sessions, thereby creating a built-in time to work on that transition. The following are some examples of transition training programs used during the base preparation phase (all done at O_2 intensity level). Each fulfills various physiological, nutritional, psychological, and musculoskeletal needs and provides an array of benefits, all of which target the important specifics of the bike-to-run transition:

- Longer distance (as measured in time) bike course to shorter distance run
- Shorter distance bike course to longer distance run
- Medium-distance bike course to longer distance run
- Longer distance bike course to longer distance run
- Longer distance bike course to medium-distance run
- Cross training. The base preparation phase for many athletes occurs during the cooler part of the year, so in most climates, the weather is not always conducive to training. Exercise restrictions due to the weather and the need to keep the body and spirit regenerated make base conditioning an excellent opportunity to add measured doses of cross training. While cross training with activities other than swimming, cycling, and running will not improve performance in the latter sports as well as working exclusively on those sports will, it does, nonetheless, "condition" the athlete and can offer a welcome break.

© Empics

Working transitions into your training will help you experience smooth, stress-free transitions when you race.

Table 7.1 Base Preparation Workout Overview

Week	1	2	3	4	5	6	7	8
Phase	BP16	BP15	BP14	BPr13	BP12	BP11	BP10	BPr9
Swimming Workouts	4	3	3	2	3	4	3	3–4
Swimming Targets	Test; Masters Group Swim; Flank Head-Up Kicking	Non-Freestyle; Off-Side Modified Side-Kick Stroke	Three-Touch; Masters Group Swim; IM	Biceps Rotation Elbow at Extension	Masters Group Swim; 3 to 6 × 400 LVT-a-b; Hand Atop the Wall	Power Side-Kick Switch; Forearm Flexion; Masters Group Swim	DPS; IM; Kick Sets	Hypoxic Pulling; Double-Arm Down Accelerations
Biking Workouts	3	3	4	3	3	3	4	1–2
Biking Targets	Ascending and Descending OLS; High-RPM 95 to 100 spinning; Low-RPM Flats With Aero Bars or Pace Line Intervals	Long Aerobic Climb, Low-RPM; Flats With Aero Bars; High-RPM 100 to 110 on Moderate Rolling Terrain	High-RPM Climbing; Standing Core Drill; Test	VMO; Transition; High-RPM Climbing	Sectors; Stand Up and Sit Downs	Group Fartlek; High-Low-RPM Switch	High-Low-RPM Switch; Long Aerobic Climb, Low-RPM	O_2 Mixed Terrain
Running Workouts	3	4	3	3	4	3	3	1–2
Running Targets	Track Drills	Stadium Stair Hops; Test	Power Hike/Run	Dynamic Ankle Calisthenic and Technical Drill Fartleks	3-Day Drills	Reduced Support Phase Long Hill	Heel Under; Stadium Stair Hops	Medicine Ball Lunges; LVTa Transition
Transitions	No	No	No	O_2 bike to O_2 run	No	No	O_2 bike to O_2 run	O_2 bike to LVT-a run
Cross Training	Optional	Optional	Optional	Yes	Optional	Optional	Optional	Yes
Dryland Phase	A	A	A	E	B	B	B	E
Dryland Volume (hours)	1:45	2:15	2:00	1:15	2:15	2:30	2:15	1:30
Dryland Upper-Body Workouts	2	1	2	1	2	2	2	1
Dryland Lower-Body Workouts	1	1	2	1	1	2	2	1
Core Workouts	2	3	3	2	4	3	2	1
Flexibility Workouts	3-4	5	4	5	3-4	4-5	4-5	5-7

9	10	11	12	13	14	15	16
BP8	BP7	BP6	BPr5	BP4	BP3	BP2	BP1
4	3	3	2	4	3	3	1–2
High Flexed Elbow, Open Armpit; Masters Group Swim; Fingertips Down, Palm Back; Test	Masters Group Swim; High Flexed Elbow, Open Armpit	Freestyle 3 to 6 × 500 LVT-b Forearm Flexion; Masters Group Swim	High Flexed Elbow, Open Armpit; Low Hand, High elbow	Low Hand, High Elbow, Masters Group Swim; Individual Medley	Open-Water Workout; Masters Group Swim; Armpit, 6-Beat Kick, Power Side-Kick Switch	Non-Freestyle; Biceps Rotation; Flank Heads Up Swimming; Masters Group Swim	Power Side-Kick Switch; Forearm Flexion; Test
3	4	3	3	4	3	4	3–4
Stand Up and Sit Downs; Long Aerobic Climb, Low-RPM; High-RPM Climbing	Rollers VMO; Long Aerobic Climb, Low-RPM	High 105 to 110 RPM; High-RPM 100 Pace Line; Test	Turbo (Roller) Transitions; High-RPM Climbing	High-RPM Pace Line; Long Aerobic Climb, Low-RPM; Rollers VMO	Long Aerobic Climb; Low-RPM Pace Line Intervals; Rollers One-Legged Spinning and Sectors	Stage Week (Rolling/ Climbing) With Bunched Workouts; High-RPM Climbing	Stage Week (Flats and O$_2$ Mixed Terrain)
3	3	4	2	3	4	3	1–2
Calm Eyes; Track Drills; Long Hill	Reduced Support Phase; Test	Quick Feet; Pawing (Full-Foot Prancing); Stadium Stair Hops; Test	Long Hill	Hands to Hips High-Knee Skips; Course Profile	Hands to Hips High-Knee Skips; Quick Feet; Long Hill	Pawing Accelerations; Reduced Support Phase	Track Drills; Course Profile
No	No	O$_2$ bike to O$_2$ run	LVT-a bike to O$_2$ run	No	LVT-a bike to LVT-a run	LVT-b bike to LVT-a run	No
Optional	Optional	Optional	Yes	Optional	Optional	Optional	Yes
A	A	A	E	B	B	B	E
2:15	2:30	2:15	1:30	1:00	1:15	1:15	0:45
1	2	2	1	3	3	2	NA
2	1	1	1	1	2	2	NA
3	3	4	2	3	3	3	2
4	4	5	5–7	5	5	5	5–7

- Supplemental phase. Each periodization phase (i.e., "BP1") corresponds with a particular supplemental dryland phase. The exercises and definitions are found in chapter 5.
- Dryland volume. This is the total dryland volume (expressed as time) for the week.
- Dryland upper-body workouts. This is the total number of upper-body workouts for the week.
- Dryland lower-body workouts. This is the total number of lower-body workouts for the week.
- Core workouts. This is the number of abdominal and stability "core" workouts for the week.
- Flexibility workouts. This is the number of stretching or flexibility workouts for the week.

Volume and Intensity

The volume of training undertaken during the base preparation phase is determined as a percentage of the total season volume. Table 7.1 illustrates how the volume can be established for each sport for the overall 16-week period. The program total volume in table 7.2 is derived from the total season training volume in table 6.7 (page 139).

Table 7.2   Base Preparation Training Volume

	Swimming	Cycling	Running	Dryland
Season total volume	200,000 m	175 h	120 h	38.25 h
Base preparation total volume	105,000 m	106 h	64.5 h	28.5 h
Base preparation % of total volume	53%	53%	54%	75%
Weeks 1–4, % of base preparation total	20%	20%	20%	25%
Weeks 5–8, % of base preparation total	25%	25%	25%	30%
Weeks 9–12, % of base preparation total	30%	30%	30%	30%
Weeks 13–16, % of base preparation total	25%	25%	25%	15%

A unique feature of my work is how I manage the intensity of training for each discipline (see table 7.3). Each week, a volume is assigned to each training intensity level. Base preparation training includes far fewer upper-level intensity workouts than the race preparation phase does.

You'll notice in table 7.3 that much of the base preparation phase follows a traditional three-week buildup followed by a one-week restoration. The basis for this approach is twofold.

First, the training overload from the three-week buildup makes a cycle of rest essential so the body can achieve progress in conditioning.

Second, it is during the restoration period that this training progression takes place.

In my experience, this three-to-one structure works best for most individuals, helping them build their conditioning and prevent injury and burnout from steady, intense training. Still, if you want to alter this setup, you can as long as you allow for a recovery phase after any build-up cycle, the lengths of which will depend on the fitness of the athlete and his or her ability to overload and recover from workouts. The longest build-up cycle I recommend is five weeks, although I know some triathletes who have successfully used a build-up to recovery cycle of one to one, two to one, and even four to one. A combination of these cycles may also work for you. The important thing is that you include some kind of recovery week during which training is lower in volume and intensity at least every five weeks.

As a final point, note that overtraining is detrimental to the body's ability to compensate and reduces training progression. Training hard is important for reaching your peak level of ability, but triathletes often walk a fine line beyond which one too many workouts at volume or intensity levels that are too high can result in crossing that line and needing to take off days, weeks, or even months to recuperate. Pay very close attention to how your conditioning is developing and build in periodic restoration breaks.

Workout Targets

As noted previously, during base preparation the training focus is primarily on developing general aerobic preparation and conditioning, improving exercise economy by drill training, increasing muscle length (flexibility), increasing general and specific strength, stabilizing the core, and undergoing professional analyses of your swimming, cycling, and running techniques.

A good way of ensuring that the training objectives are being met throughout the phase is to set weekly workout targets for swimming, cycling, and running. These benchmarks provide a point of concentration in every week. Here are a number of base preparation targets I've used for each sport during the 16-week base periodization phase. The triathlete can include one or more targets for each week's swimming, cycling, or running.

Swimming Targets

Flank Head-Up Kicking. This is a three-part target, with each part benefiting different aspects of swimming mechanics: body rotation, pulling, and kicking. During the flank target, work on getting as much as possible of the flank of your body out of the water during the recovery phase of the stroke. The head-up focus is met by doing one or two main sets during which your head is out of the water for several

Table 7.3 Base Preparation Intensity Periodization

Week	BP16	BP15	BP14	BPr13	BP12	BP11	BP10
Swimming (volume in m/% of volume of total phase)							
Total	**5,100**	**5,500**	**7,100**	**3,500**	**6,000**	**7,000**	**8,500**
Zone 1 O$_2$	3,800 75%	3,600 65%	4,200 60%	3,300 95%	4,800 80%	7,000 100%	6,000 70%
Zone 2a LVT-a		800 15%	1,400 20%		1,200 20%		2,100 25%
Zone 2b LVT-b		800 15%	1,100 15%				
Zone 2c LVT-c	1,300 25%						
Zone 3 VO$_2$		300 5%	400 5%				400 5%
Zone 4 LAC				200 5%			
OD	1,000 20%	1,400 25%	1,100 15%	1,800 50%	900 15%	1,100 25%	900 10%
Cycling (volume in h:m/% of volume of total phase)							
Total	**4:15**	**5:00**	**6:00**	**3:21**	**5:15**	**6:15**	**7:54**
Zone 1 O$_2$	4:15 100%	4:00 80%	4:30 75%	3:15 97%	4:00 75%	4:00 65%	4:45 60%
Zone 2a LVT-a		1:00 20%	0:30 10%		1:15 20%	1:15 20%	2:00 25%
Zone 2b LVT-b			1:00 15%			1:00 15%	0:45 10%
Zone 2c LVT-c							
Zone 3 VO$_2$							0:24 5%
Zone 4 LAC				0:06 3%			
OD	1:30 38%	2:00 40%	2:45 45%	1:15 35%	1:45 35%	2:30 40%	3:30 45%
Running (volume in h:m/% of volume of total phase)							
Total	**3:00**	**3:15**	**4:15**	**2:23**	**3:45**	**4:15**	**5:15**
Zone 1 O$_2$	3:00 100%	2:45 80%	3:30 85%	2:15 95%	3:45 100%	3:45 90%	4:30 85%
Zone 2a LVT-a		0:15 10%	0:45 15%			0:30 10%	0:45 15%
Zone 2b LVT-b							
Zone 2c LVT-c		0:15 10%					
Zone 3 VO$_2$							
Zone 4 LAC				0:08 5%			
OD	1:00 35%	1:30 40%	2:00 45%	0:45 35%	1:15 35%	1:45 40%	2:15 45%

BPr9	BP8	BP7	BP6	BPr5	BP4	BP3	BP2	BPr1
4,500	**7,500**	**8,500**	**10,500**	**5,500**	**6,000**	**7,200**	**8,500**	**4,500**
4,300 95%	6,000 80%	6,400 75%	7,300 75%	5,200 95%	4,500 75%	4,600 65%	5,100 60%	3,400 75%
		2,100 25%	3,200 30%			1,100 15%	1,700 20%	
					1,500 25%	1,100 15%	1,300 15%	
	1,500 20%							1,100 25%
						400 5%	400 5%	
200 5%				300 5%				
1,100 25%	1,500 20%	2,100 25%	1,600 15%	2,800 50%	900 15%	1,400 20%	900 10%	2,300 50%
4:08	**6:30**	**7:30**	**9:15**	**4:39**	**5:15**	**6:15**	**7:45**	**4:00**
4:00 97%	5:15 80%	6:00 80%	7:30 80%	4:30 97%	4:00 75%	5:00 80%	5:45 75%	3:00 75%
	1:15 20%	1:30 20%	:52:30 10%		1:15 25%		2:00 25%	1:00 25%
			:52:30 10%			1:15 20%		
0:08 3%				0:09 3%				
1:15 30%	1:45 25%	2:15 30%	3:15 35%	1:30 30%	1:15 25%	2:00 30%	2:45 25%	1:15 30%
2:39	**4:45**	**5:15**	**6:30**	**3:11**	**3:45**	**4:15**	**5:15**	**2:45**
2:30 95%	3:30 75%	3:30 65%	5:00 75%	3:00 95%	2:45 75%	3:30 80%	4:00 75%	2:00 75%
	0:45 15%	1:00 20%	1:30 25%		1:00 25%		1:15 25%	0:45 25%
		0:30 10%				0:45 20%		
	0:30 10%	0:15 5%						
0:09 5%				0:11 5%				
0:45 30%	1:15 25%	1:30 30%	2:15 35%	1:00 30%	1:00 25%	1:15 30%	1:45 35%	0:45 30%

strokes either on prescribed laps or at your own choosing. The kicking set is one of long-distance interval kicking performed without a kickboard. Vary the kicking positions from prone and supine to the right side and left side. The kick constantly works the upper thighs; keep your ankles and toes relaxed and loose.

Non-Freestyle. Emphasize more off-stroke training along with drills during this week. Butterfly, backstroke, and breaststroke training are excellent "cross training" and help improve the hands' and forearms' freestyle feel for the water.

Three-Touch. Complete a long training set (500 meters straight swim) doing the three-touch drill (touching your hand to your hip upon exit then your armpit during the recovery, and finally, the forehead during each stroke). This is an excellent drill for developing body rotation and coordination of the above-water arm biomechanics. An option would be to complete one or two of the above during the swim.

Off-Side. For an entire workout, swim breathing either on your weak side or bilaterally. Off-side breathing is an excellent technique for developing skills for open-water swimming in windy conditions or surf.

Individual Medley. During this week, swim 80 percent of one workout non-freestyle (back, breast, and fly).

Biceps Rotation. Rotate the biceps muscles inward following the entry and extension phases. This helps achieve the much-needed high elbow position during the initial part of the stroke.

Elbow at Extension. For the full workout, position your forearm and head so you can see the tip of your elbow when your arm is fully extended following entry. Keep your armpit open while you move your fingers, hand, and forearm downward during the positioning phase of the stroke.

Masters Group Swim. Join a masters workout to improve your skill before your speed and work on drafting the swimmer in front.

3 to 6 × 400 LVT-a-b. In one workout this week, swim three to six 400s at LVT-a to LVT-b intensity. Allow 30 seconds' rest between each swim and decrease your time in each 400. Endurance athletes should consider longer distance (300, 400, 500, and 1,000 meters) interval swimming as a mainstay in their training.

Power Side-Kick Switch. Push from the wall onto your side with your left hand at extension and your right hand on your thigh. Kick vigorously in an arrow, streamlined body position for one-half of the length, then switch by stroking powerfully onto your other side. During the switch, hold the extension until the recovering hand is just about to enter the water before beginning the stroke. This drill teaches you how to coordinate the kick while holding the extending arm at the surface of the water.

Forearm Flexion. Following entry, extension, and gliding onto your side, "flex" your forearm and hand back toward your chest and across your abdomen. This is a critical move for maintaining a high elbow position and promoting peak propulsion.

Kick Sets. One workout during this week should highlight kicking drills both with and without a kickboard and swim fins. Swim fins, by the way, tend to diminish coordination of the kick and arm motions. I therefore don't recommend using fins during workouts. Kick sets are fine, but most of the kicking should be done without fins. Some kicks to practice are the supine (on your back), fly, backstroke, lateral (on your side), prone (on your belly), and vertical (perpendicular to the surface of the water) kicks. Each of these can be done without a board and fins.

Distance Per Stroke (DPS). Count the number of strokes you take over the course of several lengths while you warm up and calculate the average number per lap. For the rest of the workout, reduce this number by one and hold to that throughout the workout. This is not an easy drill, but it helps to elongate the underwater stroke, relax the kick to lessen a constant "boiling" of the water, and streamline the body on its side axis.

Hypoxic Pulling. Use a pull buoy and swim training paddles (I recommend the Speedo Swimfoil Paddles) to promote diagonal strokes and optimally shape the hand pathway. Although the benefits and risks of breath holding while swimming are not fully understood, I believe that there are certain benefits in training to remain calm and maintain the most efficient stroke mechanics when your oxygen intake is reduced. However, I do not recommend that you hold your breath for a longer amount of time than is comfortable for you. Swim a long, straight set of series of 200 repeats, breathing each third, fifth, seventh, and ninth time. Your pace will have to be slow so you can avoid taking an extra breath before the ninth one.

Fingertips Down, Palm Back. A week of swimming using this technique will make you a better swimmer. Simply keep your fingertips pointing toward the bottom of the pool throughout the underwater stroke.

Double-Arm Down Accelerations. Take two powerful strokes with your right arm and then two with your left. Allow your body to rotate with each stroke. As you position your hand and "anchor," begin accelerating the speed of the stroke. For example, perform a set of $12 \times (25$ drill, 25 swim, 25 drill, 25 swim).

High Elbow, Spiral Kicks. Following the entry and catch, maintain a high elbow position for beginning the downsweep. Then flip onto your back and spiral kick for several seconds with your hands overhead. Rotate fully to the left and then return to swimming on your back. Rotate to the right and return again to your back. Focus on kicking throughout the drill.

Low Hand, High Elbow. The elbow is the first part of the arm to exit the water upon completing the stroke. Continue moving your elbow high, but keep your forearm and hand "low," near the side of the body, during the recovery.

High Flexed Elbow, Open Armpit. During each swim in this week, concentrate on maintaining a high elbow position with your arm flexed and your armpit open during the entire stroke. To do this, imagine that you have a tennis ball under your armpit; at no time during the stroke should you feel your armpit squeezing the ball. You will feel the elbow exceptionally high as the hand and forearm sweep through the stroke. This is perhaps the most important stroke technique you can continue to develop because it places your hand in the most potentially propulsive and lift-generating position along with using a larger group of muscles during the stroke.

Open-Water Workout. With a group of friends, swim an open-water course in a series of intervals and repeats. Practice sighting, rounding, and head-up strokes.

Hand Atop the Wall. Picture yourself swimming over a wall. That is, at entry, place each hand, palm down, atop the imaginary wall. Keep your hand there while you "lift" your body over your hand and the wall. To do this, keep your elbow higher than your hand throughout the stroke.

Modified Side-Kick Stroke. Kick on the right side for a three-count stroke and move onto the left side for another three-count stroke. Your belly button will face the side of the pool if you've done the movement correctly.

Cycling Targets

Descending and Ascending One-Legged Spinning (OLS). OLS drills are an excellent choice for learning the correct pedaling action. Decreasing OLSs are performed, for example, beginning with 20 OLSs with the right leg and 20 with the left, and ending with 1 right- and 1 left-leg spin. Increasing OLSs are the opposite, beginning with 1 right-leg and 1 left-leg spin and ending with, for example, 20 right-leg and 20 left-leg spins. Refer to chapter 3 for more on this drill.

Low-RPM Flats With Aero Bars. During this workout, hold the rpm at 75, usually in the large chainring. Remain in the aero bars the entire time on flat to rolling terrain. Work the over- and downstrokes during this drill.

High-RPM Climbing. In the small chainring and low gear, maintain at least 90 rpm for 15 to 45 minutes (or longer) during a challenging uphill climb.

High-RPM 100+. This involves spinning at 100 rpm or greater for the full workout regardless of terrain. Refer to the High Revolutions Per Minute drill in chapter 3 for more information.

VMO Squat. In the vastus medialis oblique (VMO) drill, you use a pedaling technique that teaches you to "engage" the medial (inward) quadriceps muscle of the thigh while you pedal. During the overstroke, push forward and downward on the pedals using the inner thigh muscles.

Transition. Simulate a bike-to-run transition at the indicated intensity zones.

Sectors. Train the downstroke, backstroke, upstroke, and overstroke in prescribed workouts. For example, go 4 × 2 minutes at each sector. Refer to chapter 3 for more on this drill.

Standing Core. Rise off the saddle for extended periods regardless of the terrain. Begin with 2, 3, 5, and then 10 minutes out of the saddle and eventually work your way up to 20 minutes or more. Refer to chapter 3 for more on this drill.

Group Fartleking (Change of pace training). As you cycle in a group of three to five triathletes, randomly change the pace and leader, but always stay together (drafting). That is, don't lose anyone from the group. If you're too fast for others, spin at a low gear or work on drills or your body position to match the speed of the group. The pace will fluctuate depending on who is leading, but the leader must pay attention to keeping the group together.

High-Low-RPM Switch. Spin at high rpm (100) for 30 seconds, then switch gears to low rpm (75) for 30 more seconds. Repeat this for 5 to 20 minutes.

O_2 Mixed Terrain. Perform a long aerobic conditioning workout ride on varied terrain, concentrating on spin mechanics and body posture. Maintain the same intensity on all terrains (uphill, flat, and downhill).

Stand Up and Sit Downs. Rise out of the saddle and make three to five strokes just after shifting two gears higher. Then shift two gears lower and sit back down for 30 strokes. Repeat for 5, 10, or 15 minutes.

Rollers or Trainer VMO. Ride for 30 minutes on the rollers or a trainer, with each pedal stroke focused on the forward and downward pass through the downstroke. Every five minutes, do the following:

  • VMO Squat (chapter 5). Go 2 × 15 seconds hold and 15 repetitions.

- High RPM Ups and Downs. Stand up and sit down every five seconds while maintaining a high rpm for one minute.
- High RPM. Go 100+ rpm in a small chainring.

Turbo (Roller) Transitions. For this workout, warm up for 15 minutes by spinning, then quickly dismount, change into your running shoes, and run for one minute at VO_2 pace. Then go for five minutes at a low rpm on the bike at your LVT-a pace with one minute VO_2-pace run transitions.

High-RPM Pace Line. In a small group of two to four riders, agree to maintain a constant pace to keep the group intact. Every rider will be in a small chainring drafting just behind the rider in front (6 to 12 inches). The leader stays in front for 30 to 60 seconds, then slides to the left, slows, and falls behind the last rider.

Long Aerobic Climb, Low rpm. Bike for one hour or longer for a climbing O_2 to LVT-a, working the downstroke in a stable body position (ears over shoulders, chest up, chin up) in a high gear at an rpm of 70 to 75.

Low-RPM Pace Line Intervals. Bike in a small group of two to four riders, with each triathlete working at 70 to 75 rpm for the entire workout. Try the following:

- LVT-a (zone 2a) at a high rpm in a small chainring with each rider leading for 15 minutes.
- LVT-b (zone 2b) 40K race-pace effort with each rider taking the lead for four minutes.

Stage Week (Rolling/Climbing) With Bunched Workouts. During this week, take four to six rides that are aerobic, drill-based, and over rolling terrain, with one or more 30-minute aerobic climbs. Two or more consecutive days of rides are bunched (two or more cycling days in a row). This target is well suited for long-distance triathletes.

Stage Week (Flats). During this week, take four to six rides that are aerobic, drill-based, and over flat terrain.

Running Targets

Track Drills. Warm up for 12 minutes at O_2 pace, stretch for 5 minutes, 8 × (15 seconds high-knee, sideways, and backward skipping, form accelerations), O_2 pace for 12 minutes.

Calisthenic and Technical Drill Fartleks. During an overdistance aerobic run, pause every 10 minutes for 2 minutes of dryland exercises (VMO Squats, push-ups, forward and reverse lunges, Single-Legged Squats, stretching, and so on). Or, include High-Knee Skipping, Kick-Ups, or other drills.

Stadium Stair Hops. Flex your knees and hop two-legged or single-legged up two stair steps for 3 to 10 steps (repeat other leg if done single) and 2 to 4 sets. Or hop up three steps on both or a single leg for 3 to 5 repetitions. At the top of the staircase or at each level, do 10 push-ups.

Power Hike/Run. For 20 to 30 minutes, hike briskly on cross country trails over hills and peaks, carrying a daypack. Then run for 5 to 10 minutes (O_2). Repeat this sequence for one to four hours or more.

Dynamic Ankle Stabilization. Every 20 minutes during an overdistance run, spend 5 minutes walking on the balls, heels, inner sides, and outer sides of your feet.

Three-Day Drills. On three consecutive days, go to the track and perform 30 to 45 minutes of running drills such as: 8×20 seconds each prancing, dynamic ankle walking (balls, heels, inner sides, outer sides), sideways running, high knees, and form accelerations.

Reduced Support Phase. The less time the foot remains in contact with the ground, the greater the horizontal velocity for the runner. Make an effort during foot strike to move off your foot quickly following support and stance.

Heel Under (Reduced Lever). Following the foot strike, bring your heel up under your buttocks more directly by reducing the rearward swing of the leg.

Long Hill. To develop aerobic strength, run a long uphill for 20 to 60 minutes at O_2 (zone 1) to LVT-a (zone 2a).

LVT-a Transition. Following the bike segment, make an immediate transition to the run in zone 2a (LVT-a).

Overdistance With Lunges (Forward and Backward). After every 15 minutes of an overdistance run, do one to three sets of 10 forward and 5 backward walking lunges. Bring the knee high during the forward lunge to a full extension with the supporting leg. Then squeeze the transverse abdominals while bringing the support leg and knee forward and upward for the next lunge.

Medicine Ball Lunges (Forward and Backward). With a 1- to 5-kilogram medicine ball held overhead, lunge forward six times with your right and then your left leg. Then reverse the lunges to go backward. Another option is to bring your knee up to the "march" position briefly before making the lunge.

Calm Eyes. For the entire week, maintain "calm eyes," be tension free, and do not focus too narrowly on any objects.

Stairs. At a stadium, run up the stairs, taking one or two stairs at a time for two minutes. Then run 400 to 800 m (O_2) on the track, incorporating high-knee skipping along the straightaway. Repeat this three to six times.

Quick Feet. With low knee lift, make short, quick strides and remain relaxed with smooth arm swings. Imagine running across a trampoline or a bed of hot coals, just touching the surface with each foot.

Uphill Pace Line. With a group of 3 or 4 friends, run single file uphill for 30 to 60 minutes. The leader dictates the pace, but must not lose the last runner. Each runner will lead for an interval of one minute before going to the rear.

Hands to Hips High-Knee Skips. While executing exaggerated high-knee skipping, bring your hands to the tops of your hips each time and recover by allowing your arms to swing forward and upward. Perform these for 1 of every 10 minutes during an overdistance run.

Course Profile. Run the course or simulate the profile of the first triathlon event of the season.

Pawing (Full-Foot Prancing). In at least two workouts this week, do the following during the warm-up: the prancing drill (quick, light steps) with "full-foot" contact with the ground. At each foot strike, "paw" backward and bring the heel up quickly toward the buttocks.

Pawing Accelerations. While running, emphasize "grabbing" the ground with the foot during foot strike in a "pawing" manner while the body moves over the foot. Go 50 m pawing while accelerating running speed every 10 m. Execute every 15 minutes for four 50 m repetitions.

CHAPTER 8

Base Transition Phase

The base transition phase focuses on more sport-specific training and increases the overall volume of work, the number of transitions (bike-to-run workouts) drilled, and the workout intensity. The phase is four weeks in length and consists of three build-up weeks and one restoration week. As described in chapter 6, several build-up and restoration combinations are possible throughout the season. This phase's transition from base preparation is gradual, but it prepares you for more sharpening and the higher-intensity workouts that start in the next phase: race preparation (see chapter 9). The fourth week is a restoration week, providing you with just the right amount of rest before the first week of race preparation training.

It is during this transition period that your body and mind become more alert and attuned to the upcoming racing season. Particular benefits from the training done during this phase include:

- Increased endurance and connective tissue growth
- Progressive increases in volume and specific training intensities, including LVT, VO_2, and LAC training
- Increased transitions and development of lung, muscular, and race-specific (bike-to-run) adaptations
- Additional strength, mobility, flexibility, and neuromuscular coordination

Workout Plan

Your highest weekly training volume of the season is reached during this phase. It is important, therefore, to have had a solid base preparation phase in which you gradually built up your fitness to be able to handle this volume and stay healthy. Without an adequate periodization of base training, there is not as much likelihood that you will accomplish what you want to in your races.

As with the base preparation phase, this phase uses a workout table that shows an overview of the entire phase (see table 8.1) broken into weekly workouts (number, types, and intensities) and targets for swimming, cycling, running, and supplemental training. You may adapt the table according to how your assessment and testing results are evaluated.

Table 8.1   Base Transition Workout Overview

Week	1	2	3	4
Phase	BT4	BT3	BT2	BT1 (recovery)
Swimming Workouts	3	3	3	2
Swimming Targets	Masters Group Swim; Moderate VO_2	Double-Arm Down Accelerations—Masters Group Swim	A.M./P.M.; Masters Group Swim; Non-Freestyle	Test; Drills: Catch Up Freestyle, Distance per Stroke
Biking Workouts	3	3	4	2
Biking Targets	Standing Core Drill	Long Aerobic Climb High-RPM; Low-RPM Flats With Aero Bars	Stage Week (Flats)	Test (LVT-a/b)
Running Workouts	4	4	3	2
Running Targets	All Track Drills Week	Cross Country OD + 20–40 min Uphill LVT-a to LVT-b	3 × Track Drills	Balke Test or 5–10K LVT-b
Transitions	No	Yes	No	No
Cross Training	Optional	Optional	Optional	Yes
Dryland Phase	B	C	C	E
Dryland Volume (hours)	1:00	0:45	0:45	0:45
Dryland Upper-Body Workouts	1	2	2	1
Dryland Lower-Body Workouts	1	2	2	0
Core Workouts	3	3	1	3
Flexibility Workouts	4–5	4–5	4–5	5–7

As in the base preparation phase, periodic testing is essential to objectively measure your progress in training. For swimming, I generally use a 500- to 1,650-yard (400 to 1,500 m) time trial at LVT-c pace. For cycling, a 5-, 10-, or 15-mile time trial at LVT-c pace provides a good standard. For running, a 5K time trial is a good bet. The distance you choose for each test should depend on your workout volume and event goals.

The swimming, cycling, and running targets are training suggestions that add a "training relationship" to the phase by including certain specifics in one or more workouts. The table also notes guidelines for transitions, cross training, and dryland training (phase, volume, and workouts for core strength and flexibility).

Volume and Intensity

The volume of base transition workouts is a percentage of the total season volume selected by the triathlete. Again, I believe it's important to follow a closely managed volume and intensity framework to maximize performance and to minimize injury and musculoskeletal overuse problems. Table 8.2 details the training volumes for swimming, cycling, and running during the base transition phase. Note that it is during this phase that you will accumulate the longest swimming, biking, and running volumes of the training season.

Table 8.2   Base Transition Training Volume

	Swimming	Cycling	Running	Dryland
Season total volume	200,000 m	175 h	120 h	38.25 h
Base transition total volume	30,000 m	26.25 h	18 h	3.25 h
Base transition % of total volume	15%	15%	15%	8%
Weeks 1–4, % of base transition total	100%	100%	100%	100%

While training volume management is essential to achieving your best results, it is perhaps even more important to manage the volume of the intensity of training. Table 8.3 demonstrates how this is easily managed for swimming, cycling, and running. I believe it is important to manage the total weekly volume of workouts in each intensity zone and the overall training volume to achieve optimal performance levels. You do not need to be too narrowly focused on volume and intensity, but having a standard will help you develop a progressive workload in both intensity and training volume. In other words, it will help you make certain that neither too much nor too little volume and intensity are carried out in training. Note that the overdistance percentages in the table are based on a percentage of the total weekly volume and are not part of the intensity percentages.

Table 8.3 Base Transition Intensity Periodization

Week	BT4	BT3	BT2	BTr1
Swimming (volume in m/% of volume of total phase)				
Total	**7,000**	**8,000**	**10,000**	**5,000**
Zone 1 O_2	4,200 60%	4,000 50%	5,500 55%	3,500 70%
Zone 2a LVT-a	1,400 20%	1,400 17%	1,300 13%	
Zone 2b LVT-b	1,400 20%	2,000 25%	2,500 25%	
Zone 2c LVT-c				1,500 30%
Zone 3 VO_2		400 5%	400 4%	
Zone 4 LAC		200 3%	300 3%	
OD	1,400 20%	2,000 25%	2,500 25%	1,300 25%
Cycling (volume in h:min/% of volume of total phase)				
Total	**6:00**	**7:00**	**9:00**	**4:30**
Zone 1 O_2	5:30 90%	5:30 80%	6:15 70%	4:00 90%
Zone 2a LVT-a	0:30 10%	1:30 20%	1:45 20%	
Zone 2b LVT-b			1:00 10%	
Zone 2c LVT-c				0:30 10%
Zone 3 VO_2				
Zone 4 LAC				
OD	2:30 40%	2:45 40%	3:30 40%	1:15 30%
Running (volume in h:min/% of volume of total phase)				
Total	**4:15**	**4:45**	**6:00**	**3:00**
Zone 1 O_2	3:00 70%	3:45 80%	4:45 80%	2:45 90%
Zone 2a LVT-a		1:00 20%	1:15 20%	
Zone 2b LVT-b	0:45 20%			
Zone 2c LVT-c	0:30 10%			0:15 10%
Zone 3 VO_2				
Zone 4 LAC				
OD	1:30 35%	2:00 40%	2:45 45%	1:00 35%

Workout Targets

Apply these workout targets to specific workouts or as a general guide/focus during each week of the base transition phase. The following are four targets each for swimming, cycling, and running, corresponding to each of the four weeks in the base transition phase.

Swimming Targets

Masters Swim Week (Moderate/VO$_2$). Swim each of this week's workouts with your masters group. After two workouts, swim a set of 2 to 3 × 200 at VO$_2$ pace). Your effort should be at a slightly faster pace than for a 1,650/1,500 race.

Two-Armed Pulls and 1 × Masters. Do two-armed pull (double arm down) drills in each workout. Swim with the masters group once this week to work on drafting and head-up freestyle.

A.M. and P.M. Swims. For two days, swim at a morning drill workout and in the evening with your masters group.

Test and Drill Training. Complete a swim time trial. In a long-course pool or open water, do an LVT-b continuous swim. Work on sculling, hip rotation at extension, and a forceful downbeat kick during the initial phase of the underwater stroke.

Cycling Targets

Standing Core and Long Overdistance. During each workout in this week, include overdistance work and stand out of the saddle for a period of 5, 10, or up to 20 minutes. Regardless of the terrain, remain standing.

Long Climb to Short Run Transition. Choose a long hill that will take 30 to 60 minutes to climb. Before you start, park your car at the top. After you bike to the summit, transition into a short 20- to 40-minute run at LVT-a level.

Bike Stage Week. Complete four to five bike workouts this week. Include two technical drill training sessions, one group workout, one overdistance workout, and one morning and evening workout in your plan.

LVT-a-b Time Trial. Choose a course with a profile and distance similar to that of your first race of the season. Ride this course hard at just above LVT-a, but not quite at LVT-b.

Running Targets

All Drills Week. Include in every workout high knees, kick-outs, prancing, single-legged drills, and form accelerations for 15 to 20 minutes.

Cross Country and Uphill All Week. Do every workout during this week on trails. One workout is 20 to 40 minutes uphill.

3 × Drills. Run three consecutive days performing these drills as follows: 8 × 20 seconds of high knees, dynamic ankle walking, kick-ups, sideways and backward kick-outs, and skipping.

Balke or 5K to 10K Road Race Test. Target a Balke test or road race and compete at LVT-b.

CHAPTER 9

Race Preparation Phase

The race preparation phase prepares you for competition. Swimming, cycling, and running workouts are highly specific in race-pace intensity and race volume. The dryland component of training also changes, with intensity increasing while volume decreases (i.e., heavier weight, added resistance, and fewer repetitions). Specificity, too, is essential as key competitions draw near. The workouts are dedicated to helping you develop the greatest physical condition possible. To do so, workouts more often replicate race intensity and sometimes even race distance. The volume of work done in intensity zones 2c, 3, and 4 also increases.

Transition workouts also intensify and increase in number during this eight-week stage. The main training objective is to boost your training upper limit to close to peak levels, that is, the threshold at which you can maintain race-pace intensity for the longest period of time.

Other objectives include:

1. Increasing training for race specificity and intensity by
   - adding LVT-b and -c training,
   - increasing the number of transition workouts,
   - increasing the volume and number of maximal oxygen uptake workouts ($\dot{V}O_2$max), and
   - increasing the volume and number of anaerobic capacity training workouts (LAC).

2. Reducing overall training volume to
   - increase confidence as training speed progresses, and
   - focus on cognitive competitive strategies.

Cognitive Strategies: Achieving a Desired Outcome

Successful races require extraordinary commitment. Competing with the sole purpose of finishing the race, placing high, or winning is more likely accomplished as a result of your mind commanding your body than by your body alone. In the end, what your mind and inner voice say are usually obeyed by your body.

My 20-some years of working with triathletes have resulted in a significant portion of my work on the mental aspects of competition. Performance anxiety, compulsive disorders, self-confidence and self-esteem issues, chronic fatigue, depression, anger, and fear of failing and of success are just some of the difficulties that a sport performance coach encounters. When an athlete gets on my "coach's couch" (as they often do), I listen attentively to every word they say, but perhaps more importantly, I keep in my mind the outcome they want to realize, or rather fear they may not realize.

In psychology there is a technique called *cognitive behavior therapy* that works quite well in most circumstances that involve some kind of conflict. I have the athlete describe what actually happened (the result) in the situation he's concerned about by setting the scene and not going into many personal details of what was said or thought. Then, after reviewing the circumstances, the athlete describes the self-talk he experienced in these circumstances. After that, I ask this yes-or-no question: "Was your desired outcome achieved?" If the answer is "yes," there's no problem. If the answer is "no," we move on to the final step, in which the athlete visualizes and describes a completely new but similar scenario in which the outcome desired is accomplished.

I have seen this process work wonders for many people. We all at one time or another face some degree of self-doubt, experience disappointing events, and the like, but overcoming them by using this technique doesn't happen with just one rehearsal. It takes much practice (just like training) to achieve a positive outcome, which, of course, is everyone's goal. I always tell my athletes to pursue that by making each moment and movement better than the last.

© Empics

Workout Plan

Using table 9.1 can help you determine the number of weekly swimming, biking, running, transition, dryland, core, and flexibility workouts. As with the corresponding tables for the previous two phases (chapters 7 and 8), the suggestions I make in table 9.1 can be modified according to the results of the assessments you made during base preparation testing and your fitness, race goals, and, of course, time availability. I like the lead-in to the first competition of the year to consist of eight weeks of race preparation training. After that, the program often moves more or less from recovery-restoration to another series of race preparation weeks and peaking before the next competition. If there are five weeks between the first and second events, the week after the first one will be for restoration, the following two or three weeks for race preparation, and the last week for peak transition.

Volume and Intensity

The race preparation volume, like the previous phases, is determined as a percentage of the total season volume (chapter 7). Typically, an eight-week race preparation period equals about 25 percent of the total annual training volume. Table 9.2 illustrates the volume for this phase.

As with the two previous phases (base preparation and base transition), the overall and intensity volumes continue to follow a prescribed periodization (table 9.3). Race-specific intensities and the volumes of higher-intensity forms of training will increase.

Workout Targets

The following weekly targets are used to assist in designing workouts for athletes. The targets blend with the periodization by providing overall training goals for the week. The following are for the race preparation phase and begin with the first week of the eight-week phase.

Swimming Targets

Masters Swim Week (VO$_2$). Swim each of this week's workouts with your masters group. After two workouts, swim a set of 2 to 4 × 200 VO$_2$. The efforts are slightly faster than the race pace for the 1,650/1,500.

Open-Water Group Swim (LVT-a). Swim the equivalent event time at LVT-a for the race distance.

Test. Test yourself in a 400 m to 1,650-yard race at LVT-c.

Long Course. Do one long-course (50 m pool) technique workout and one overdistance swim.

Table 9.1 Race Preparation Workout Overview

Week	1	2	3	4	5	6	7	8
Phase	RP8	RP7	RP6	RPr5	RP4	RP3	RP2	RPr1
Swimming Workouts	4	2	3	2	4	2	3	2–3
Swimming Targets	2 × Masters Group Swim; Quality VO$_2$ Freestyle 2–4 × 200	Open-Water Workout; Technical Drills	Forearm Flexion; Flank Head-Up Kicking; Test	Long Course (low volume)	High Quality, Masters Group Swim + LAC 4–8 × 50	6 × 500 Long Course	LVT-b 2 × 300, 400, 500	VO$_2$ + Open-Water Workout
Biking Workouts	3	4	3	2	2	4	4	3
Biking Targets	LVT-b Test; Long Aerobic Climb, Low RPM; Flats, HRPM at 95 RPM	VO$_2$ Hill Repeats, Low-RPM Pace Line, Flats; Rollers	Over-Distance, High-RPM Group Pace Line, Rolling Fartleking	LVT-b Test; Low Week Volume	High-RPM Climbing; Test	LVT-b Course Profile (75%)	LVT-b Course Profile (70%)	LVT-c Transition; VO$_2$ Hill Repeats; Test
Running Workouts	4	3	4	2	4	4	3	3
Running Targets	Track: VO$_2$ and LAC Sets + Drills	Track: VO$_2$ and LAC Sets + Drills + Transition	Balke Test or 5–10K LVT-b/c	2 × Drills, Cross Country, LVT-b Fartleking (low volume)	Track: LVT-b 2–4 × 2,000 + 1 min, 10 min Drills, LACs	Fartleking: LVT-a 3–6 × 4 min + 1 min; or Track: VO$_2$/LAC	Track: Drills 15–30 and LAC Sets + 5K Test	Track or Fartleking: LVT-b 4 × 4 min + 30 sec, 10 min Drills or Jog, VO$_2$ 2–3 × 5 + 5
Transitions	LVT-a bike to LVT-a run	No	No	LVT-b bike to LVT-b run	No	No	O$_2$ long bike to LVT-a run	LVT-c bike to LVT-c run
Cross Training	Optional	Optional	Optional	Yes	No	No	No	No
Dryland Phase	D	D	D	E	D	D	E	N/A
Dryland Volume (hours)	1:00	1:00	0:45	0:30	0:45	0:45	0:30	N/A
Dryland Upper-Body Workouts	1	2	1	1	2	2	1	0
Dryland Lower-Body Workouts	1	2	0	0	2	1	1	0
Core Workouts	3	2	3	3–4	3	3	2	1
Flexibility Workouts	4–5	4–5	4–5	6–7	4–5	4–5	4–5	5–7

Table 9.2   Race Preparation Training Volume

	Swimming	Cycling	Running	Dryland
Season total volume	200,000 m	175 h	120 h	38.25 h
Race preparation total volume	50,000 m	43.5 h	29 h	5.25 h
Race preparation % of total volume	25%	25%	25%	14%
Weeks 1–4, % of race preparation total	55%	55%	55%	60%
Weeks 5–8, % of race preparation total	45%	45%	45%	40%

Masters Swim Week (LAC). Swim each workout with your masters group and add a set of LAC 4 to 8 × 50 plus one to two minutes of rest.

Open-Water Group Swim (LVT-b). Swim the equivalent event time at LVT-b for the race distance.

300s, 400s, and 500s (LVT-b). Two workouts during this week should consist of LVT-b sets of 2 to 4 × 300, 400, and 500 m at short send-off intervals (30 seconds) and decreasing the 100 m average pace for each swim.

High-Intensity VO_2 Set. Early in the week, do one set of VO_2 swims following a 20-minute warm-up, with 2 to 5 × 200 plus rest interval equaling swim time.

Cycling Targets

Time Trial (Flats to Hill Climb). LVT-b to -c time trial performed with 80 percent of the distance over flats and finishing with a hill climb.

VO_2 Hill Repeats. On a hill that takes 4 to 10 minutes to climb (or turn around at that point), repeat a set of 2 to 4 × at VO_2 pace.

Flat Low-RPM and Hill High-RPM. On flat terrain, ride in the large chainring at a low rpm of 75 to 80. On hilly terrain, stay in the small chainring at a high rpm of 90 to 100 or more.

LVT-b Time Trial. If you have previously recorded a course time try to improve by 10 to 30 seconds only. Don't try to set a new time record by more than this because the test is a bridge to other tests that follow.

High-RPM Hill Climb and Drills. Complete one hill climb at 90 to 105 rpm. Also do two sessions of 10 to 20 minutes of drill training (single-legged spinning, sectors, and accelerations).

Simulate Course Profile (LVT-b) and Intervals. Ride a course similar to that for the target, completing several LVT-b intervals such as 5 × 5 minutes plus a one-minute rest.

Table 9.3 Race Preparation Intensity Periodization

Week	RP8	RP7	RP6	RP5	RP4	RP3	RP2	RP1
Swimming (volume in m/% of volume of total phase)								
Total	**6,500**	**7,500**	**9,100**	**4,500**	**5,100**	**6,000**	**7,600**	**4,000**
Zone 1 O_2	2,100 32%	2,800 37%	3,800 42%	4,300 95%	1,500 30%	2,100 35%	3,000 40%	1,200 30%
Zone 2a LVT-a								
Zone 2b LVT-b	2,600 40%	3,000 40%	3,600 40%		1,300 25%	1,200 20%	1,500 20%	800 20%
Zone 2c LVT-c	1,300 20%	1,100 15%	900 10%		1,800 35%	1,800 30%	1,900 25%	1,200 30%
Zone 3 VO_2	300 5%	400 5%	500 5%		500 10%	600 10%	800 10%	600 15%
Zone 4 LAC	200 3%	200 3%	300 3%	200 5%		300 5%	400 5%	200 5%
OD	1,300 20%	1,900 25%	1,400 15%	2,300 50%	800 15%	1,200 20%	1,500 20%	600 15%
Cycling (volume in h:min/% of volume of total phase)								
Total	**5:21**	**6:27**	**7:54**	**4:05**	**4:36**	**5:09**	**6:23**	**3:14**
Zone 1 O_2	2:15 43%	2:45 42%	3:30 45%	3:10 78%	2:15 48%	2:30 47%	4:15 68%	1:30 48%
Zone 2a LVT-a	1:07 20%							
Zone 2b LVT-b	1:08 20%	2:30 40%	3:30 43%	0:50 20%	1:45 40%	1:45 35%	2:00 30%	0:45 25%
Zone 2c LVT-c	0:45 15%	1:00 15%	0:45 10%		0:30 10%	0:45 15%		0:45 20%
Zone 3 VO_2		0:12 3%				0:09 3%		0:14 7%
Zone 4 LAC	0:06 2%		0:09 2%	0:05 2%	0:06 2%		0:08 2%	
OD	2:45 50%	3:00 45%	3:15 40%	2:00 50%	2:15 50%	2:15 45%	2:30 40%	1:15 40%
Running (volume in h:min/% of volume of total phase)								
Total	**3:57**	**4:14**	**5:32**	**2:39**	**2:39**	**3:42**	**3:52**	**1:59**
Zone 1 O_2	2:00 50%	2:15 55%	3:15 60%	2:30 95%	1:15 45%	1:45 45%	2:00 50%	0:45 40%
Zone 2a LVT-a	0:45 20%	1:15 30%	0:30 10%		0:30 20%	1:15 35%	0:30 14%	
Zone 2b LVT-b	1:00 25%		1:30 25%		0:45 30%		1:00 25%	0:30 25%
Zone 2c LVT-c		0:30 10%				0:30 15%		0:30 25%
Zone 3 VO_2	0:12 5%		0:17 5%		0:09 5%		0:14 7%	0:14 10%
Zone 4 LAC		0:14 5%		0:09 5%		0:12 5%	0:08 4%	
OD	2:00 50%	2:00 45%	2:15 40%	0:45 25%	1:15 45%	1:30 40%	1:15 30%	0:45 30%

LVT-b Course Profile. Ride a bike course similar to the race's course but 30 to 70 percent of the distance.

LVT-c to VO$_2$ Hill Repeats. LVT-c and VO$_2$ hill repeats of two to eight minutes. The number of repetitions is determined by training volume. Generally, the triathlete will go 2 to 6 repetitions of two minutes and 1 to 2 repetitions of eight minutes.

Running Targets

Track (LAC and VO$_2$). Do only one track session this week and emphasize quality form, intensity, and drills.

Balke Running $\dot{V}O_2$max Field Test. Run a Balke test or a 5K road race at LVT-b.

2 × Technical Drill, Cross Country Fartlek. Do two sessions of prancing, dynamic foot drills, high-knee skipping, sideways, backward, and kick-up drills. Also do two sessions of cross country LVT-b fartleking.

Track (LVT-b). Run at your LVT-b pace for 2 to 4 × 2,000 m plus a one-minute rest, drill for 10 minutes, then run at your LAC pace for 3 to 6 × 200 m plus 200 m walk.

Fartlek Workout. Run at your LVT-a pace for 5 × 4 minutes plus 1 minute easy running, drill or jog for 10 minutes, run at VO$_2$ pace for 5 × 3 minutes plus 3 minutes easy walking or rest.

Track. After 30 minutes of jogging, stretching, and general warming up, complete a LAC set of 4 to 6 × 200 m plus 200 m walking as form accelerations and LAC 2 to 4 × 300 m plus 1 minute walking.

Track or Fartlek. Run at your LVT-b pace for 4 × 4 minutes plus a 30-second rest, drill or jog for 10 minutes, then run at your VO$_2$ pace for 3 × 5 minutes plus 5 minutes walking.

CHAPTER 10

Peak Transition Phase

Peaking and tapering fitness for end-of-season competition is an essential piece of the successful triathlete's program. Triathletes looking to perform at their highest level for a specific competition need to plan their training so that they are well rested to peak perfectly for that race.

There are as many methods of peaking as there are coaches and athletes. Everyone seems have individualized tapering methods, and to a large extent this is as it should be. However, some of these tapering programs are sounder than others. Tapering effectively requires reducing and narrowing your physiological and psychological focuses. By reducing training volume and sharpening intensity over the course of one to three weeks, you will likely achieve a positive peak. Yet some taperings and buildups prior to competition result in dulled performance if they include too much volume too late in the phase, too much intensity too close to the competition, and not enough rest.

It is the preceding phases—base preparation, base transition, and peak transition—as well as appropriate dryland training periodization that provide the building blocks for an optimal tapering and for that peak performance. However, demonstrably sound training throughout the training years contributes more to the results than the peak and tapering phases do. Some of the objectives of a solid peak transition phase include the following:

- Enhancing energy-producing enzymes to very high levels. Essentially, reductions in overall training volume permit larger quantities of glycogen for energy to be stored in the muscles.

- Increasing blood volumes with high-intensity training to raise the quantities of oxygen and fuel that can be transported to working muscles

- Enhancing nervous and muscular system development to their peak levels with more LAC workouts

- Increasing aerobic, muscular power, and lung capacity to peak levels by increasing the volume and number of $\dot{V}O_2$max workouts

- Adding LVT-b and LVT-c training (short, high-intensity) to sharpen speed and increase muscle glycogen concentration, blood volume, and red blood cell level
- Reducing overall training volume to facilitate an increase in the quality of workouts
- Increasing confidence as training speed progresses
- Focusing on cognitive competitive strategies

In short, peaking for a competition will ready you physiologically and psychologically, as well as sharpen your body for peak performance. Muscular power will increase, blood lactate levels will lower, and nervous and muscular system function will improve.

The peak transition period continues for one to three weeks, depending on the length of the competition and your athletic shape (see table 10.1).

Table 10.1   Recommended Tapering Times

	World Class	Top Amateur	Good Amateur	Average Amateur	Beginner
Sprint to Olympic	3–5 days	4–5 days	4–5 days	7 days	7 days
Half-Ironman	7 days	7–14 days	14 days	7–14 days	7–14 days
Ironman	21 days	21 days	14–21 days	14–21 days	7–21 days

Planning the Peak Transition Phase

In this final section of the training program, you once again organize the number of workouts for swimming, cycling, running, dryland training, and transitions. During this final period, the workouts are shortened and their intensity increases beyond race pace for many of the workouts. Table 10.2 details how this is managed for this particular period.

Peak Transition Training Volume and Intensity

The start of peaking actually begins during the fifth week of the race preparation phase. At that point, total training volume is reduced while intensity and race specificity increase week by week through the end of the race preparation phase. Of course, there are many individual variables that go into determining the right format for tapering. A professional or top age-group triathlete whose buildup has been interrupted by injury, illness, or other

Table 10.2   Peak Transition Workout Overview

Week	1	2	3
Phase	PT3	PT2	PT1
Swimming Workouts	4	3	3
Swimming Targets	Open-Water Workout or Long Course	LVT-b 400s	VO$_2$ day 1–2; LAC day 6
Biking Workouts	3	4	2
Biking Targets	LVT-b/c, Uphill or Fats	Transition LVT-c/c	Fartlek LVT-b/c
Running Workouts	3	4	4
Running Targets	LAC 3–6 × 200 m + 200 m Walk; Double-Arm Down Accelerations; LAC 2–4 × 300 + 1 min	LVT-b 1–4 × 800–1,200 m; 10 min Track Drills; VO$_2$ 2–3 × 800 to 1,000 m	VO$_2$ 400–1,000 m; Jog/Walk 3–5 min; LAC 2–4 × 200 m + 200 Walk
Transitions	No	LVT-c bike to LVT-c run	No
Cross Training	No	No	No
Dryland Phase	D	E	N/A
Dryland Volume (hours)	0:45	0:30	0
Dryland Upper-Body Workouts	1	1	0
Dryland Lower-Body Workouts	1	0	0
Core Workouts	3	0	1
Flexibility Workouts	5–7	5–7	5–7

training detours might taper for one week before an Ironman competition, as might a beginner triathlete with a limited athletic history preparing for her first Ironman. In both cases, prolonged tapering isn't necessary since the fitness level of each of these athletes would not endure the high-intensity intervals associated with a typical taper. Of course, reducing the peak phase to one week means that there will be one or more additional weeks in the race preparation phase, but the additional training volume during the third and, to some extent, second weeks before the event would help the athletes in our example to develop more aerobic fitness.

Training programs, periodization, and tapering are all factors that should be individualized for each athlete; there are just too many variables for the one-size-fits-all approach to coaching that has gained popularity on the Internet to be successful. Following a sound program, even if it is generic, does have value, but keep in mind that the best programs are those that can be customized to fit your needs.

Table 10.3 provides an overview of the swimming, cycling, running, and dryland workouts for a three-week peak transition phase. If you are tapering for only two weeks, start with the two-weeks-before the race volumes. If you're tapering for only one week, start with the one-week-before volumes.

Table 10.3   Peak Transition Training Volume

	Swimming	Cycling	Running	Dryland
Season total volume	200,000 m	175 h	120 h	38.25 h
Peak transition total volume (including race event)	15,000 m	12.25 h	7.75 h	1.5 h
Peak transition % of total volume	7%	7%	6%	3%
3 weeks from race, % of peak transition total	40%	50%	50%	80%
2 weeks from race, % of peak transition total	30%	30%	30%	20%
1 week from race, % of peak transition total	30%	20%	20%	0%

Like the previous periodization chapters, the peak transition phase follows a format for managing the type and volume of intensity (table 10.4). This, of course, is of particular importance during the final buildup to the event—and a "buildup" is what I like to call it, not a complete rest period for tapering. As Scott Tinley and I often discussed prior to events, I like my triathletes to be on the upswing of training just before the competition. This means sharpening the body for racing.

Table 10.4 Peak Transition Intensity Periodization

Week	PT3	PT2	PT1
Swimming (volume in m/% of volume of total phase)			
Total	**7,100**	**4,000**	**4,000**
Zone 1 O$_2$	3,500 50%	1,600 40%	2,000 50%
Zone 2a LVT-a			
Zone 2b LVT-b	1,100 15%	600 15%	1,400 35%
Zone 2c LVT-c	1,400 20%	1,200 30%	
Zone 3 VO$_2$	700 10%	400 10%	400 10%
Zone 4 LAC	400 5%	200 5%	200 5%
OD	3,500 50%	1,600 40%	2,000 50%
Cycling (volume in h:min/% of volume of total phase)			
Total	**6:03**	**3:50**	**2:39**
Zone 1 O$_2$	3:15 55%	2:15 57%	1:30 59%
Zone 2a LVT-a			1:00 35%
Zone 2b LVT-b	1:30 25%	0:30 15%	
Zone 2c LVT-c	1:00 15%	0:45 20%	
Zone 3 VO$_2$	0:11 3%	0:12 5%	0:06 4%
Zone 4 LAC	0:08 2%	0:08 3%	0:03 2%
OD	3:00 50%	1:30 40%	2:30 100%
Running (volume in hours:min /% of volume of total phase)			
Total	**3:32**	**2:31**	**1:38**
Zone 1 O$_2$	1:45 50%	1:00 40%	0:45 45%
Zone 2a LVT-a			0:15 16%
Zone 2b LVT-b	0:30 15%	0:30 20%	0:30 30%
Zone 2c LVT-c	0:45 20%	0:45 30%	
Zone 3 VO$_2$	0:21 10%	0:11 7%	0:06 6%
Zone 4 LAC	0:11 5%	0:05 3%	0:02 3%
OD	1:45 50%	1:00 40%	1:00 55%

Peak Transition Workout Targets

The training targets during peak transition shift toward reduced volume, increased intensity, and more rest days. Depending upon the length of the competitive event, peak transition periods last from one to three weeks.

The following weekly targets are used to assist in designing workouts beginning with the third week from the event. The targets blend with the periodization by providing overall training goals for the week.

Swimming Targets

Open-Water Group Swim (LVT-b). Three weeks before the event, swim the event equivalent time (LVT-b) for the race distance.

300s, 400s, and 500s (LVT-b). During the second week prior to the event, do two workouts consisting of LVT-b sets of 2 to 4 × 300, 400, and 500 m at a short sendoff interval (30 seconds) and decreasing the 100 m average pace for each swim.

VO_2 Set Day 1 or 2 and LAC Day 6. Early in the week prior to the event, after a 20-minute warm-up, do one set of VO_2 swims of 2 to 5 × 200 plus rest interval equaling swim time. These efforts should be of a high intensity and controlled (not sprints). The day before the event complete a set of LAC swims, do 4 to 6 × 50 with a 2:1 or 3:1 work: rest ratio.

Cycling Targets

Simulate Course Profile (LVT-b) and Transition (LVT-c) (3 weeks from event). Ride a course similar to the race course—25 to 50 percent of the distance.

LVT-c Transition (2 weeks from event). Complete a bike-to-run transition workout at LVT-c intensity. Depending on event distance the LVT-c portion of cycling time would be between 10 and 25 minutes.

Fartlek Zones 2b, 2c, and 3 (1 week from event). LVT-b, LVT-c, and VO_2 zones as part of a fartlek change of pace interval workout.

Running Targets

Track Workout. Three weeks before the event, following 30 minutes of jogging, stretching, and general warming up, complete a LAC set of 4 to 6 × 200 m + 200 m walking as form accelerations, LAC 2 to 4 × 300 meters + 1 minute walking.

Track Workout and Transition. Two weeks from the event, run at LVT-b for 4 × 800 to 1,200 m + 30 seconds rest, drill or jog for 10 minutes, then run at VO_2 for 3 × 800 to 1,000 m + 5 minutes walking. For the transition workout, run at LVT-c for 12 to 15 minutes.

Track or Fartlek (Change of Pace). One week before the event, following a warm-up and stretching, run at VO_2 for 800 to 1,000 m, then jog or walk for 3 to 5 minutes. Then run at LAC 2 to 4 × 200 m + 200 m walking.

CHAPTER 11

Race Day Readiness

The days before a competition are filled with anticipation, mounting energy, and an eagerness to put to use all the training preparation that has come before. At no triathlon is this more apparent than at Ironman Hawaii, the World Series of triathlon. Most participants want to hit their peak in fitness on this day.

Yet what was included in the tapering phase profoundly impacts your state of mind. Triathletes who are confident, rested, and have stuck to an appropriate periodization and build-up schedule are more likely to feel ready and secure come race day. This final chapter examines the days leading up to a competition like Ironman Hawaii, but it could just as easily be a regional event, an Olympic distance, a sprint event, your very first race, or a triathlon of any distance. I present some psychological methods for you to practice prior to the event and discuss in general swimming, biking, and running workouts and nutrition in the days leading up to an event, the race day plan, and my thoughts on good and not so good races.

Psychological Preparation

The nights and quiet times prior to competition are valuable times for training with cognitive skills that will enhance performance. I like my triathletes to daydream about successful performances and outcomes. I also have them rehearse how they might respond to difficult situations that might take place. Both of these methods inspire positive outcomes and provide them with the tools they would have acquired if they had actually lived through an event. While the situations may not have been "real," my triathletes have nonetheless imagined the scenarios and worked through the processes and problems successfully.

Triathletes should also rehearse in their minds how the swimming, biking, and running will feel to their muscles. Doing so coaches the mind to effectively anticipate the process of starting the swim or rounding a buoy, the chaos of the swim, the transition from swimming to cycling, the long climbs and steep descents, changing a flat, the transition from cycling to running, tolerating the heat and fatigue, and eventually crossing the finish line.

Self-talk is also vitally important. Perhaps the most effective mantra I've come up with is *Make each movement better than the last.* This helps the athlete move forward after each stroke, pedal, and stride. Rather than dwelling on what may have happened or is about to happen, the triathlete moves forward in response to this "self-talk" message while the past becomes nothing and the next movements become better and better.

Finally, imagine what your absolute peak performance would feel like, an optimal competition in which you'd complete a physically and emotionally flawless race for *you*, without regard to the competition or end result.

© Martina Sandkuhler/Jump

Use positive self-talk and visualize your optimal performance in the days before your big event.

Three Days Before

You are not going to become any more fit during the last few days before the competition. You can become more fatigued, though, so the final three days before an event is no time to work too hard. A few key workouts are just what you'll need to feel your body and mind peaking at the right time. In my programs, all of the workouts are customized to the individual throughout the season. The specific volumes, drills, intensity levels, and days of training are sequentially outlined. What follow are some of the details of what you should consider during the final days leading up to a competition.

Workouts

Do a couple of workouts on this day—swimming and running. Start with a 500 to 1,500 m easy warm-up, kicking, and drills. Then do a set of two or three 200s at VO_2 pace followed by a 200 or 300 m of freestyle and non-freestyle swimming to cool down. Finally, end the swim workout with two to six 25 m LAC repeats. The running workout typically is an easy jog of 10 to 20 minutes followed by a concentrated 20 to 30 minutes of stretching.

Nutrition

First, there are some hard and fast rules about nutrition. Here are the top ten principles (in no particular order) for training and preparing for competition.

1. Eat breakfast every day, especially before early-morning workouts. Missing breakfast is an enormous mistake because, simply put, it reduces the number of calories you will have available for energy. Low blood sugar saps mental and physical energy by causing the body to rely heavily on proteins and fats as the chief fuel source. In addition, if you're trying to lose weight, any calories you "saved" by skipping breakfast are often gained back by bingeing or overindulging later in the day, especially in the evening. If you (like me) cannot stomach foods early in the morning before workouts, try eating a banana and some yogurt or have a sports drink so you take in 200 to 400 calories.

2. Drink vast amounts of water. A rule of thumb for determining the amount is one liter for each hour of exercise or 1,000 calories expended. You're drinking enough if you have the urge to urinate every two or three hours.

3. Consume foods and nutrients that you are familiar with. Doing otherwise can create havoc in the upper and lower gastrointestinal tracts (bloating, cramps, gas, and diarrhea). Find a combination of foods that works for you before a major competition and stick to it. It's also a good idea to eat and drink what the race organizers will provide for long-distance events.

4. Bonking, or "hitting the wall," is often temporary, as long as there are energy sources available. Your muscles don't run out of glycogen for the most part, but your brain does because it needs carbohydrates to function properly. Recognize, then, that when you feel weak, light-headed, or sluggish while training or racing, it generally means you're off track with your nutritional intake. Eating will restore your blood and liver glycogen stores, and within a short time your energy level will recover.

5. Enzymes that make glycogen are most receptive to carbohydrate replenishment immediately following exercise. I recommend consuming

at least 50 to 100 grams of carbohydrate in the 15 to 30 minutes immediately following exercise.

6. Consume a varied diet of green leafy vegetables, fruits, fresh fish (omega-3 fatty acids found in salmon help reduce inflammation and encourage recovery from exercise), free-range meat and dairy products, whole grains, nuts, and olive or canola oils. These foods are pretty basic and easy to prepare; stay away from packaged and canned foods.

7. Be sure to replenish your protein stores with at least 60 to 100 grams of protein (more when you're injured) every day so you can rebuild on a daily basis.

8. Vitamin supplementation for the most part is unnecessary if you have a sufficient and uniform diet. However, if you are dieting, a vegan, pregnant, have allergies, or are lactose intolerant, you may have persuasive reasons for supplement use. There are some vitamins and mineral supplements that may have some added benefits, but for the most part, they are not needed. However, if you eat a well-balanced menu, drink plenty of fluids, and still don't recover from events or training or experience chronic illnesses (colds) or overtraining conditions, supplementation with vitamins C, D, and E, zinc, calcium, or iron may be called for. Last, know that if the claims of a supplement seem too good to be true, they *are!*

9. Wash your hands often when you're preparing and eating foods. Avoid catching colds by practicing sound cleanliness and avoiding public situations that might bring you in contact with people and their runny noses. Remember, too, that the better the diet you eat is, the stronger your immune system will be.

10. Here's the recipe for my favorite snack. Blend or mix together the following for a great treat.
    - Plain nonfat yogurt (1 to 2 cups)
    - Raisins (1/4 cup)
    - Banana (1/2)
    - Toasted soy nuts, unsalted (1/8 cup)
    - Raw pumpkin seeds, unsalted (1/4 cup)

Table 11.1 estimates the total calories or grams of carbohydrates, protein, and fat you should consume per kilogram or pound of your body weight three days before the event.

Table 11.1 Caloric Intake Three Days From Competition

Body Weight		Carbohydrate (7 g/kg)		Protein (1.7 g/kg)		Fat (0.9 g/kg)		Total
(kg)	(lb)	(g)	(cal)	(g)	(cal)	(g)	(cal)	(cal)
45	99	315	1,260	76.5	306	40.5	162	**1,728**
47	103	329	1,316	79.9	319.6	42.3	169.2	**1,805**
49	108	343	1,372	83.3	333.2	44.1	176.4	**1,882**
51	112	357	1,428	86.7	346.8	45.9	183.6	**1,958**
53	117	371	1,484	90.1	360.4	47.7	190.8	**2,035**
55	121	385	1,540	93.5	374	49.5	198	**2,112**
57	125	399	1,596	96.9	387.6	51.3	205.2	**2,189**
59	130	413	1,652	100.3	401.2	53.1	212.4	**2,266**
61	134	427	1,708	103.7	414.8	54.9	219.6	**2,342**
63	139	441	1,764	107.1	428.4	56.7	226.8	**2,419**
65	143	455	1,820	110.5	442	58.5	234	**2,496**
67	147	469	1,876	113.9	455.6	60.3	241.2	**2,573**
69	152	483	1,932	117.3	469.2	62.1	248.4	**2,650**
71	156	497	1,988	120.7	482.8	63.9	255.6	**2,726**
73	161	511	2,044	124.1	496.4	65.7	262.8	**2,803**
75	165	525	2,100	127.5	510	67.5	270	**2,880**
77	169	539	2,156	130.9	523.6	69.3	277.2	**2,957**
79	174	553	2,212	134.3	537.2	71.1	284.4	**3,034**
81	178	567	2,268	137.7	550.8	72.9	291.6	**3,110**
83	183	581	2,324	141.1	564.4	74.7	298.8	**3,187**
85	187	595	2,380	144.5	578	76.5	306	**3,264**
87	191	609	2,436	147.9	591.6	78.3	313.2	**3,341**
89	196	623	2,492	151.3	605.2	80.1	320.4	**3,418**
91	200	637	2,548	154.7	618.8	81.9	327.6	**3,494**

Two Days Before

The day that is two days prior to a competition typically is a day off from training. This day is often filled with last-minute preparations, registration, bike check-in, and sorting clothes, food, and other race-day items, as well as time for rest. It is also a good day to have an early-evening or late-afternoon dinner and "taper" your activities as the night comes.

Workouts

Since there are no workouts on this day, *rest* becomes the primary goal along with stretching for an extended period or multiple sessions. Don't start in on a muscle-lengthening program or decide to get a massage if you haven't been doing so on a regular basis. Do, however, gently stretch the major areas of the body as detailed in chapter 1 and treat these as workouts. In other words, they are important!

Nutrition

This is the best day for big carbohydrate loading. That is, your meal or meals should be fairly high in carbohydrates (70 percent) and low in fats and proteins. By the way, triathletes should "load" daily during training. This does not mean that you should ignore fats and proteins altogether, but a high percentage (60 to 70 percent) of your diet should be composed of carbohydrates to ensure that you have adequate muscle glycogen and to promote recovery from training.

Table 11.2 estimates the total calories or grams of carbohydrates, protein, and fat you should consume per kilogram or pound of your body weight two days before the event.

One Day Before

I love this day. It's when every competitor's energy is at its highest. There is no more time for ruminating about how much, how little, how often, and what kind of training has or has not been done. The day before a competition is the day before truth. There is no more "dig me" beach time (a term used by the locals in Kona in reference to the triathletes who hang out at the swim start in the days before the race); people are peacefully introspective, having lost their shells of bravado. The day before a competition is a great time to be a coach, because you can see your triathletes glow in what they've become and what they are about to find out about themselves.

Table 11.2 Caloric Intake Two Days From Competition

Body Weight		Carbohydrate (10 g/kg)		Protein (1.4 g/kg)		Fat (0.8 g/kg)		Total
(kg)	(lb)	(g)	(cal)	(g)	(cal)	(g)	(cal)	(cal)
45	99	450	1,800	63	252	36	144	2,196
47	103	470	1,880	65.8	263.2	37.6	150.4	2,294
49	108	490	1,960	68.6	274.4	39.2	156.8	2,391
51	112	510	2,040	71.4	285.6	40.8	163.2	2,489
53	117	530	2,120	74.2	296.8	42.4	169.6	2,586
55	121	550	2,200	77	308	44	176	2,684
57	125	570	2,280	79.8	319.2	45.6	182.4	2,782
59	130	590	2,360	82.6	330.4	47.2	188.8	2,879
61	134	610	2,440	85.4	341.6	48.8	195.2	2,977
63	139	630	2,520	88.2	352.8	50.4	201.6	3,074
65	143	650	2,600	91	364	52	208	3,172
67	147	670	2,680	93.8	375.2	53.6	214.4	3,270
69	152	690	2,760	96.6	386.4	55.2	220.8	3,367
71	156	710	2,840	99.4	397.6	56.8	227.2	3,465
73	161	730	2,920	102.2	408.8	58.4	233.6	3,562
75	165	750	3,000	105	420	60	240	3,660
77	169	770	3,080	107.8	431.2	61.6	246.4	3,758
79	174	790	3,160	110.6	442.4	63.2	252.8	3,855
81	178	810	3,240	113.4	453.6	64.8	259.2	3,953
83	183	830	3,320	116.2	464.8	66.4	265.6	4,050
85	187	850	3,400	119	476	68	272	4,148
87	191	870	3,480	121.8	487.2	69.6	278.4	4,246
89	196	890	3,560	124.6	498.4	71.2	284.8	4,343
91	200	910	3,640	127.4	509.6	72.8	291.2	4,441

Workouts

Training should be light, but I do prescribe that most athletes do something in all three disciplines today. Swimming and running for 10 to 15 minutes each and up to 30 minutes of cycling are sufficient. I also generally have my triathletes perform several LAC workouts of 20- to 30-second intervals with rest intervals of two or three times that long. Do the workouts early in the day, when you'll be free from anxiety; make time for rest and relaxation.

I do not recommend having a massage on this day unless it is given by a therapist you have been seeing regularly. Otherwise, doing so may cause muscle soreness and even injury. Whether it is a massage, food, vitamins, or some other performance enhancer you want to try the day before the race, don't do anything that will impact the race unless it is something that you have tried well in advance or that is a normal part of your training and tapering process.

Nutrition

Eat the largest meal at midday to ensure complete digestion before the morning of the race. Eat a wholesome selection of carbohydrates, fats, and proteins. Overeating in one or another food group can lead to gastrointestinal problems on race day. The last meal of the day should be about the amount of your normal evening meal, with perhaps a snack before bed. Drink plenty of water (do not bloat), reduce or abstain from alcohol consumption, limit high-fiber foods and sugar substitutes, and be sure to eat from the food groups you are most comfortable with. This is not the time to experiment with out-of-the-ordinary gastronomic choices.

Table 11.3 estimates the total calories or grams of carbohydrates, protein, and fats you should consume per kilogram or pound of your body weight one day before the event.

Race Day

Come race morning for events like Ironman Hawaii, it's an early wake-up call. For Dave Scott and me in 1983, it was 4:00 A.M. when I heard him and some friends outside the condominium veranda as he was warming up! Warming up is important even for an event of that distance.

Warm-Up

Gently warming the muscles raises the metabolism by enhancing fuel breakdown and increases muscle temperature for increased muscle elasticity and circulation. The warm-up also prepares the triathlete psychologically as he readies his body, checking that all the systems are ready to go.

Table 11.3   Caloric Intake One Day From Competition

Body Weight		Carbohydrate (9 g/kg)		Protein (1.1 g/kg)		Fat (0.7 g/kg)		Total
(kg)	(lb)	(g)	(cal)	(g)	(cal)	(g)	(cal)	(cal)
45	99	405	1,620	49.5	198	31.5	126	**1,944**
47	103	423	1,692	51.7	206.8	32.9	131.6	**2,030**
49	108	441	1,764	53.9	215.6	34.3	137.2	**2,117**
51	112	459	1,836	56.1	224.4	35.7	142.8	**2,203**
53	117	477	1,908	58.3	233.2	37.1	148.4	**2,290**
55	121	495	1,980	60.5	242	38.5	154	**2,376**
57	125	513	2,052	62.7	250.8	39.9	159.6	**2,462**
59	130	531	2,124	64.9	259.6	41.3	165.2	**2,549**
61	134	549	2,196	67.1	268.4	42.7	170.8	**2,635**
63	139	567	2,268	69.3	277.2	44.1	176.4	**2,722**
65	143	585	2,340	71.5	286	45.5	182	**2,808**
67	147	603	2,412	73.7	294.8	46.9	187.6	**2,894**
69	152	621	2,484	75.9	303.6	48.3	193.2	**2,981**
71	156	639	2,556	78.1	312.4	49.7	198.8	**3,067**
73	161	657	2,628	80.3	321.2	51.1	204.4	**3,154**
75	165	675	2,700	82.5	330	52.5	210	**3,240**
77	169	693	2,772	84.7	338.8	53.9	215.6	**3,326**
79	174	711	2,844	86.9	347.6	55.3	221.2	**3,413**
81	178	729	2,916	89.1	356.4	56.7	226.8	**3,499**
83	183	747	2,988	91.3	365.2	58.1	232.4	**3,586**
85	187	765	3,060	93.5	374	59.5	238	**3,672**
87	191	783	3,132	95.7	382.8	60.9	243.6	**3,758**
89	196	801	3,204	97.9	391.6	62.3	249.2	**3,845**
91	200	819	3,276	100.1	400.4	63.7	254.8	**3,931**

The duration of the warm-up depends on the athlete: In general, the greater the training volumes were leading up to event day, the longer the warm-up time will be. If you do not warm up, you undoubtedly will be slower until your muscle temperature rises and reduces cohesion and stiffness. For the most part, warm-up durations of 6 to 12 minutes in each discipline are advisable (when the weather cooperates) for competitions from the Olympic to Ironman distance. For some participants, however, warm-up may be as long as 20 to 30 minutes if the athlete noted in training that it took that long before the muscles felt fluid.

Without question, in cold-water events (even with wetsuits) I want my triathletes to stretch for at least 15 to 20 minutes and to warm up in the water. This period is vital for double-checking your ability to handle the temperature and getting your body and mind ready for a cold swim. Timing is important, because a prolonged wait before the race starts could cause a drop in the core temperature of an athlete who's left the water and is standing around waiting. Therefore, before the race, confirm the start time and ensure that your body temperature will warm up by moving about once you leave the water.

Race-Day Nutrients

Eat your precompetition meal three or more hours prior to any Ironman event. For shorter competitions such as Olympic- and sprint-distance triathlons, a full meal may be unnecessary with the typical North American early-morning race start times. In those situations, 100 to 200 grams of carbohydrates may be all that is needed. For ultradistance events, however, a carbohydrate-rich meal with low fat and protein content is recommended. In Europe, where events often begin later in the day, you can eat a more typical breakfast, but go light on the fats and proteins.

In the first 45 minutes of the hour before the race, drink as much as 40 grams of a carbohydrate sports drink. During the last 15 minutes, drink or sip only water.

During the race, your nutrient goal should be to take in 40 to 50 grams of carbohydrates each hour. This can be in a combination of sports drinks and solid foods. The fluid goal is somewhere between 16 and 30 ounces each hour. This means ingesting 4 to 8 ounces about every 15 minutes. Natasha Badmann, 2002 Ironman world champion, showed exceptional skills and adherence to fluid intake during her marathon in Hawaii. At aid stations, she would take one cup, drink some of the fluid, then take another cup and pour it into the first, pinching the top and sipping frequently (5 or 6 times) and skillfully through the station.

Professional triathletes know very well the vital importance of fluid and food intake during competition. Most have experienced decreased endurance performance and increased HR, body temperature, and RPE when nutrients were not adequate. Just a 1 percent loss in body water results in a marked reduction in maximal oxygen capacity (table 11.4), so nutrients become as central to performance as training and psychological, tactical, and technical aspects. Table 11.5 contains guidelines for ingesting fluids for events lasting more than two hours, and table 11.6 is a timetable for food ingestion for those events.

Table 11.4 Physical Symptoms and Effects of Dehydration

Body Water Lost (%)	Symptoms
1	Few signs of any thirst, but marked reduction in $\dot{V}O_2$max
2	Beginning to feel thirst, loss of endurance capacity and appetite
3	Dry mouth, impairment of performance
4	Increased effort for exercise, impatience, apathy, vague discomfort, loss of appetite
5	Difficulty concentrating, increased heart and respiratory rates, slowing of pace
6–7	Further impairment of temperature regulation, higher heart and respiratory rates, flushed skin, sleepiness, tingling, stumbling, headache
8–9	Dizziness, labored breathing, mental confusion, further weakness
10	Muscle spasms, loss of balance, swelling of tongue
11	Heat exhaustion, delirium, stroke, coma, difficulty swallowing, possibility of death

Table 11.5 Fluid Ingestion Timetable for Events Lasting More Than Two Hours

	Before Exercise	During Exercise	After Exercise
Timing and Frequency of Intake	3–6 h before competition	10–15-min intervals	First hour following exercise until partially full
Amount of Intake	16–20 oz (500–600 ml) 15–60 min before event	4–8 oz (150–250 ml)	16–32 oz (500–1,000 ml)
Carbohydrate Content	5–7% or 30–40 g per 8 oz serving	5–8% or 40–50 g per 8 oz serving	20–25% or 1.5–3 g/kg body weight

Table 11.6 Food Ingestion Timetable for Events Lasting More Than Two Hours

	Precompetition Meal	Before Exercise	During Exercise	After Exercise
Timing and Frequency of Intake	3–6 h before competition	30 min before	Hourly after first 2 h	Immediately after exercise and each 2 h thereafter
Amount of Intake (cal)	1,600–2,400	200–300	200–300	500–1,000
Types of Food	400–600 g carbohydrates plus low fats and proteins	Sport bar or sport drink and bar combination with 40 or more g carbohydrates	Sport bar or sport drink and bar combination with 40–50 g carbohydrates	High-carbohydrate replenisher with carbohydrates .07–2 g/kg body weight

Maintain Your Race Posture

If I have ever seen more perfect body posture on the run portion of a triathlon, I cannot remember when. The 2002 Ironman triathlon in Hawaii was not a record-setting day, but exceptional running form was exhibited by Peter Reid and Lori Bowden (husband and wife) with virtually indistinguishable posture. From the cervical vertebrae of the neck through the thoracic vertebrae of the middle back, their posture was a demonstration of perfection. Their necks and upper spines were arranged in a straight, balanced, and centered line, making each foot strike appear effortless, natural, and without force. This is what every runner should make an effort to achieve.

The running form of the eventual winner, Tim DeBoom, came later during the race, but his posture was confident and outstanding during the final 10 miles of the marathon. Thomas Hellriegel, who blistered the bike course and held onto the lead well into the run, showed poor running mechanics, which I believe resulted in his slower marathon time. His head swayed unsurely, of course as a result of fatigue and perhaps weak midback stabilizer muscles such as the spinal extensors. More precisely, he had not had coaching on running mechanics that encourage efficient horizontal velocity with each foot strike by maintaining a tall, centered spine. Hellriegel, a former Ironman Hawaii winner, certainly is a force in triathlon, but his pounding foot strikes and counterbalanced posture will not in the "long run" provide the best results; he must first make a few straightforward biomechanical modifications.

Finally, HR monitors are unnecessary on race day, because HR by that time carries no great weight. It's likely that at no time during the year have you been as rested as you are on race day, and HR may not be a reliable indication of effort. You therefore do not want to limit your efforts or overexert yourself based on HR data that is unreliable. RPE is your best indicator of performance, because you'll compete neither too easy nor too hard by following its guidance.

After Your Race

Whether you have what you consider a good race performance or not, you may choose to sing your own praises or tell tales of misery and bad fortune to anyone who will pay attention. Or, you may with dignity and self-respect accept your good or great performance and recognize your gifts and strengths even if things don't go as well as you had planned.

Coaching has taught me many things about myself and about mentoring athletes. I believe I spend as much time with my athletes on the psychological aspects of human growth as on training; in fact, it is probably more than one might think a coach would need to do. The relationship between the athlete and the coach typically becomes similar to that between a psychologist and a patient, but I get to torture my clients with workouts! I also get to see my clients in the real world as they interact with and react to the trials and tribulations of sport.

Winning, losing, finishing, or not finishing with "dignity and self-respect" is the most important value I can teach an athlete. In fact, as I learned with one of my athletes (Marian Davidson) at the 2002 Ironman competition, not finishing a race may well carry with it greater personal growth than finishing would have.

The disappointment was particularly hard for me since I had chosen the tires for the race. I knew that my client was at the borderline of not making the bike course cutoff time. She finished the bike course, but didn't make the time because she had two flat tires. I know, however, that the decisions I made, including my tire choice, were the best I could do at the time, and the experience taught me several coaching lessons. The biggest lesson of all came in a telephone conversation with my client the morning after the race.

She was feeling ". . . terrible . . . not good enough and worthless," she said. I told her how I had felt the night before, when I had heard from her husband that she had had flat tires and had not finished in time. I couldn't have felt worse about my decision on the tires. I told her that I even began to feel a loss of confidence in my coaching. I went on to say, however, that I had immediately switched those thoughts to marveling at how far we had come in all of the physical challenges. Not too many months before, she had lost a finger in a horseback riding accident (three others were surgically reattached), suffered a broken vertebra in another accident, and crashed on her bike during training, which led to two weeks in the hospital with cellulitis so bad she very nearly died. I told her that she had done what we set out to do, that she really had finished the bike and swim segments, and that that was amazing considering what she'd been through during the previous year.

I continued, telling her how sad and disappointed I had felt on hearing the news, but how I'd began to realize that we'd both done well in training. After all, she was in the best shape of her life and had come within a flat tire (actually she had two) of finishing. I stressed to her that others would think more of her if she held her head high, confident in knowing that she had done her absolute best. If her demeanor was proud and dignified, others would respect her and she would grow in self-respect for herself.

So she attended the awards ceremony and watched others receive medals and trophies and heard the announcer talk about being an "Ironman finisher," and it was difficult for her. She did this with the utmost confidence and respect for herself, however, and everyone she met was gracious and giving and offered her their heartfelt congratulations. On the flight home, she sat next to Chris McCormack, who also did not finish, and another woman who did not finish because her bike was involved in a collision. She later told me how both of them were positive, kind, and dignified.

There is no question in my mind that this disappointment was one of the best things to ever happen to her and perhaps to me. You see, if she'd finished, we all would have celebrated, hugged, and leaped around like a bunch of jumping beans. We would not have learned such a valuable lesson; now, when she does finish her Ironman competition, we can jump up and down, hug, and cry with dignity.

Whether you finish, win, place, improve your time, lose, or do not finish, I believe that it is vital to do so with grace and dignity. Remember: Make each and every movement and moment "better than the last."

Bibliography

Aaberg, Everett. 1998. *Muscle Mechanics.* Champaign, IL: Human Kinetics.

Applegate, Liz. 2001. *Eat Smart, Play Hard.* Emmaus, PA: Rodale.

Baechle, Thomas R. and Roger Earle. 2000. *Essentials of Strength Training and Conditioning,* 2nd ed. Champaign, IL: Human Kinetics.

Benson, Tony and Irv Ray. 1998. *Run with the Best.* Mountain View, CA: TAFNews Press.

Bompa, Tudor O. 1994. *Theory and Methodology of Training.* Dubuque, IA: Kendall/Hunt.

Brooks, Douglas. 2001. *Effective Strength Training.* Champaign, IL: Human Kinetics.

Clark, Nancy. 1997. *Sports Nutrition Guidebook,* 2nd ed. Champaign, IL: Human Kinetics.

Colwin, Cecil M. 1992. *Swimming Into the 21st Century.* Champaign, IL: Human Kinetics.

Colwin, Cecil M. 2002. *Breakthrough Swimming.* Champaign, IL: Human Kinetics.

Evans, Marc. 1997. *Endurance Athletes Edge.* Champaign, IL: Human Kinetics.

Faria, Irvin and Peter R. Cavanaugh. 1978. *The Physiology and Biomechanics of Cycling.* New York: Wiley.

Friel, Joe. 1998. *The Triathlete's Training Bible.* Boulder, CO: VeloPress

Javer, Jess. 1995. *Long Distances: Contemporary Theory, Technique and Training.* Mountain View, CA: TAFNews Press.

Jeukendrup, Asker E. 2002. *High-Performance Cycling.* Champaign, IL: Human Kinetics.

Kisner, Carolyn and Lynn Allen Colby. 1996. *Therapeutic Exercise Foundations and Techniques.* Philadelphia: F.A. Davis

Magee, David J. 1992. *Orthopedic Physical Assessment.* W.B. Saunders Company.

Maglischo, Ernest W. 2003. *Swimming Fastest.* Champaign, IL: Human Kinetics.

Martin, David and Peter Coe. 1997. *Better Training for Distance Runners.* Champaign, IL: Human Kinetics.

McArdle, William D and Frank I. Katch and Victor L. Katch. 1986. *Exercise Physiology.* Philadelphia: Lea and Febiger.

McAtee, Robert E. and Jeff Charland. 1999. *Facilitated Stretching.* Champaign, IL: Human Kinetics.

Miller, Thomas S. 2002. *Programmed to Run.* Champaign, IL: Human Kinetics.

Prentice, William E. 1990. *Rehabilitation Techniques in Sports Medicine.* St. Louis: Times Mirror/Mosby.

Sleamaker, Robert and Ray Browning. 1996. *Serious Training for Endurance Athletes.* Champaign, IL: Human Kinetics.

Weineck, Jurgen. 1986. *Functional Anatomy in Sports.* Chicago: Year Book Medical Publishers.

Index

Note: The italicized *f* and *t* following page numbers refer to figures and tables, respectively.

About the Author

Marc Evans is a pioneer in coaching endurance athletes. He got his start in 1981 when he became triathlon's first professional coach. Since then he has coached professional and age-group Ironman winners, national champions, and hundreds of other endurance athletes around the world. In addition to coaching, Evans has spread his training knowledge by authoring *Endurance Athlete's Edge* (1997). In 1989 Evans was named U.S.A. national team head coach for the first World Triathlon Championships in Avignon, France. The following year he was appointed coach of the U.S. triathlon team at the Elite Performance Testing Series held at the Olympic Training Center in Colorado Springs. Well known for his training periodization and innovative coaching methods, Evans also co-patented the SPEEDO® SwimFoil and continues to create new training techniques for endurance sport athletes of all levels.

Evans is the president of Marc Evans Coaching (www.evanscoaching.com), a sports performance company specializing in coaching individuals in swimming, cycling, and running technique and biomechanics analysis as well as providing individually tailored training and periodization plans. Clients ranging from first-time triathletes to experienced age-group and professional athletes, clubs, teams, and coaches come from around the world to work with Evans.

Evans resides in the San Francisco Bay area, where he enjoys telemark skiing, swimming, cycling, hiking with his Labradors, and playing golf.